T0013477

GOOD★SPORTS
BY GLENN STOUT

BASEBALL
HEROES

GOOD·SPORTS

BY GLENN STOUT

BASEBALL HEROES

sandpiper

HOUGHTON MIFFLIN HARCOURT
BOSTON NEW YORK

Houghton Mifflin is an imprint of
Houghton Mifflin Harcourt Publishing Company.

www.hmhco.com

The text of this book is set in ITC Slimbach.

Library of Congress Cataloging-in-Publication Data is on file.

ISBN 978-0-547-41708-0

Manufactured in the United States of America
DOC 10 9
4500678830

All photos courtesy of AP Images

This book is dedicated to

ILAN BRYANT

NICHOLAS BORTZFIELD

JOHANNES BORTZFIELD

ETHAN CRELLER

BRADY CRELLER

*and all my other young friends
and readers who are "Good Sports."*

CONTENTS

INTRODUCTION

*B*aseball has long been known as the national pastime, a game for all Americans.

Unfortunately, for many years this simply was not true. Not everyone has always been welcome at the ballpark. At various times professional baseball has either banned certain groups of people from playing or made it very, very difficult for them to play. And although America is a diverse country with people of many different ethnic backgrounds, until very recently the stands at major league ballparks have not looked like America.

Baseball Heroes tells the story of some baseball pioneers, three men and a woman—yes, a woman—who fought hard for their own right to play baseball so that everyone could participate in our national pastime. These pioneers were all "good sports" who played the game the right way and for the right reasons.

One of the first Jewish players in professional baseball, Hank Greenberg had to ignore vicious slurs and namecalling from his opponents. Jackie Robinson, the first African American to play major league baseball in the twentieth century, went through a similar experience. Mexican pitcher Fernando Valenzuela was one of the first big Latino stars in baseball and helped make the game popular with Latino fans in America. And as the first woman to play baseball both in college and professionally, Ila Borders had to convince everybody that she was good enough to play.

Each of these pioneers helped make baseball the game it is today, a game that everyone with the talent to play also has the right to play. Fans of every imaginable background turn out by the thousands to cheer their favorite teams and players. While all of these pioneers recognized that everybody is an individual and everyone is different, they also knew that in every way that is truly important, everybody is the same, and our differences should not be enough to divide us or keep us apart.

Because of them, baseball is now truly America's national pastime.

ANK GREENBERG

HANK'S LASTING LESSON

WHEN FUTURE HALL OF FAMER HANK GREENBERG took a big swing of the bat and hit the ball square, then watched the ball grow small as it soared through the air and dropped over the fence and into a sea of hands for a home run, he loved hearing the cheers of the crowd.

And when he stepped to the plate with two outs and runners on base and swung through a pitch for a strikeout, nearly falling over from the effort, he expected to hear the fans boo as he slowly walked back to the bench, dragging his bat behind him.

That was okay with Hank. Whether he was the hero or the goat, he only wanted to be judged by his performance on the field. He knew that if he accepted the cheers, he would also have to put up with the occasional jeer. That's part of playing any sport.

But there were also times when Hank Greenberg was on the field that he heard something else, not only from the fans in the stands and his opponents, but even from his own teammates, words that had nothing to do with how well he played but that attacked him for who he was as a person.

"Dirty kike!"

"Lousy sheeny!"

"Hey, Jewboy!"

When Hank was the target of taunts and insults simply because he was Jewish, he tried not to let the angry words bother him. He knew they were spoken in ignorance. If anything, such insults only made Hank more determined to do well and demonstrate by his example that Jewish athletes had just as much right to play baseball as anyone else. Each time he stepped on the baseball field, he knew that he was not just playing for himself, or his family and his team, but for all people who faced prejudice and bigotry because of their beliefs.

Hank Greenberg was born in Greenwich Village, a crowded neighborhood of immigrants, in New York City on New Year's

Day in 1911. His parents, David and Sarah, had big dreams for their son. They had both immigrated to America only a few years before from Romania in Eastern Europe. In their home country David and Sarah had both been poor, and because of prejudice against Jews they had had very little opportunity to get ahead. America, they had been told, was different, a place where people could succeed through hard work no matter what their background was.

That was true for David Greenberg. After only a few years of hard work in the United States, David started his own business, a cloth company that supplied clothing manufacturers.

But life wasn't perfect. All the Greenbergs wanted for their four children was the opportunity to send them to college. But first the children—three boys and one girl—had to get through primary school. And the Greenbergs soon learned that prejudice against Jews, known as anti-Semitism, also existed in America.

Hank Greenberg found this out while he was still young. Each morning when he prepared to leave his apartment building and walk the few short blocks to school, his stomach began to tie itself in knots. The most difficult parts of each day were his trips to and from school. He had to be careful.

As he walked down the stairs of the Greenbergs' apartment building and out onto the sidewalk, Hank would glance around nervously. Nearly every day some of the older boys in the neighborhood would lie in wait for him. Greenwich Village was a tough neighborhood anyway, but for a young Jewish boy, it was especially tough. Most of the other kids in the neighborhood were the children of Italian or Irish immigrants. They had not known many Jews before, and they were suspicious of people who were different. That was why they picked on Hank and the other Jewish children in the neighborhood.

As Hank walked down the street, he tried to be cautious, but on many occasions as soon as he turned a corner or passed an alleyway, he'd find himself surrounded by older boys.

Then it would start. One of the boys would call Hank a name.

Young Hank tried to ignore the taunts and keep walking, but then a boy would block his way. Sometimes one boy would stick out his foot while another pushed Hank from behind and sent him sprawling. Or several boys would jump on Hank's back and beat on him with their fists until he fell to the ground. Sometimes he was even beaten with a heavy woolen sock filled with stones while the boys called him names.

Hank tried to fight back, but he was usually outnumbered, and the other boys were much older and bigger. Often there was little that Hank could do but cover his head and take it, then run to school as fast as possible. And when he left school to walk home, he would have to worry about being attacked again.

That didn't stop Hank. He knew his education was important, so no matter how many times the boys came after him and how afraid he felt, Hank went to school and tried to do his best.

Still, living in fear made it difficult for Hank and the other Greenberg children to concentrate on their studies. So when Hank was seven years old, his parents moved the entire family to another section of New York: the Bronx. There were more Jewish families there, and Hank and his brothers and sister felt much safer.

On the day the Greenbergs drove uptown to their new home, Hank was excited. Not only was his new home much bigger than their old apartment, but right across the street was a huge park!

There were trees in Crotona Park, and the green grass

seemed to stretch as far as Hank could see. Even better, there were large athletic fields and baseball diamonds, and the park was full of the sounds of children playing. Hank could hardly believe it. In Greenwich Village the only place to play outside had been in the street.

Hank spent as much time as possible in the park. In the spring and summer he usually played baseball, and in the fall he and his friends would play football or soccer. When it rained or the weather was too cold to play outside, Hank went to the park recreation center and played basketball.

In fact, Hank loved playing sports so much that it soon became a problem. After school he would race right past his house, and without even changing clothes or doing his homework, Hank would toss his schoolbooks aside and start playing. Hour after hour Hank and his friends would choose sides and play one sport or another—soccer, football, baseball—sometimes all of them, one right after the other. As the sun dropped low over the park and left long shadows on the ground, Hank would race home, trying to beat his nine o'clock curfew.

David Greenberg worked long hours, but if Hank came home and saw that his father was already there, he knew what to expect. David and Sarah didn't understand how their son could be so interested in sports, particularly baseball. Hank's mother called baseball "a bum's game." The Greenbergs wanted their son to become a lawyer. Sarah and David were strict with their children, and as Orthodox Jews, Hank and the other Greenberg children had to follow rules they didn't always understand. They were not allowed to eat certain kinds of food, like pork, and other foods had to be kosher, meaning they had to be prepared under certain conditions and blessed by a rabbi, a Jewish religious teacher. Hank had to observe Jewish religious holidays, and on those days he was not allowed to participate in certain activities, such as playing in the park.

David's father was especially strict with Hank. So when Hank came home after playing at the park, he would try to sneak into the house, walking on tiptoe and slowly turning the doorknob as he entered. Hank's shirt would be dripping with sweat and his pants would be covered with grass stains. But no matter how quiet he tried to be, his father was usually waiting for him to ask if he had finished his homework. Usually, Hank's father could tell by the look on his face that he had not. No matter how tired and dirty and hungry Hank was from playing, his father would make him do his homework.

Fortunately for Hank, as long as he did well in school and faithfully followed his religion, his parents did not try to prevent him from playing. Although Hank himself would later say, "I wouldn't call myself a good student," he was bright and did well enough that his parents allowed him to continue to play sports.

Hank grew quickly, and by the time he was thirteen years old, he stood six foot three inches tall. He had bad acne and felt awkward and gawky. Other kids often made jokes about his height. He was self-conscious and easily embarrassed. He hated it when he had to stand before the class and read out loud or do a math problem on the blackboard.

Although Hank was uncomfortable with his size in the classroom, his size worked to his advantage when he played sports, particularly basketball and baseball. On the basketball court Hank towered over his opponents, and on the baseball field he was much stronger than most boys his age.

By the time he was a teenager, Hank could hit a baseball much farther than most boys at Crotona Park. Hank played first base, and his size helped him reach errant throws that smaller boys would have missed. The better he played, the more he liked the game. When he was on the baseball diamond, he didn't feel clumsy or awkward. The same kids who teased him in class slapped him on the back and cheered for him when he got a big hit. Baseball became Hank's obsession.

Hank knew about major league baseball, but even as the star of his high school team at James Monroe High School in the Bronx, he never gave professional baseball a thought. Although Yankee Stadium, home of the champion New York Yankees, was only a few miles away, he never even attended a game there.

Hank graduated from James Monroe High School a few months early, in February of his senior year in 1929, and accepted a scholarship to attend New York University to play basketball. But when spring came Hank found himself playing baseball again. Several semipro teams around New York had recruited Hank to play.

One day as Hank was practicing at Crotona Park, Pat McDonald, a former Olympian who worked out at the park almost every day and a big baseball fan, approached Hank. As Hank later told the story in his autobiography, McDonald said, "Young man, I have just come from watching the Yankees play, and you hit the ball better than Lou Gehrig."

Greenberg was stunned. Lou Gehrig, the Yankees first baseman, was one of the greatest hitters in baseball. He hit behind Babe Ruth in the Yankees lineup, and the two men made the greatest slugging combo in the history of the game. Still, if McDonald said Hank was as good as Gehrig, maybe he was! For the first time in his life, Hank began to think he might be able to play in the major leagues.

Over the next year, even as he attended classes at NYU, Greenberg continued to play semipro baseball. Major league scouts began approaching Hank to ask whether he was interested in playing professional baseball. Then the Detroit Tigers of the American League offered Hank $9,000 to turn professional—$3,000 to sign the contract and another $6,000 when he reported to the team after his freshman year of school.

Hank wanted to play. There was just one problem: his father. Hank knew how much his father wanted him to finish school.

One afternoon he met with his father and told him he had decided he wanted to play professional baseball.

His father looked at him sternly. "Pop," asked Hank, "are you against baseball as a career?" Without saying a word, his father nodded.

Hank paused for a moment and then said, "The Tigers offered me nine thousand dollars."

David Greenberg was stunned. He had never imagined that professional baseball players earned so much money. He remained silent for a long time.

"I thought baseball was a game," he said. "But now I

see that it is a business." He looked at his son. "Take the money."

Hank broke into a huge grin. He was going to play professional baseball.

When Hank signed with the Tigers, very few Jewish men had ever played in the major leagues, and none had played very long or been a big star. Many of the men who owned professional baseball teams were prejudiced against Jewish people and did not believe that Jewish people could play sports very well. These men believed in what is called a stereotype, a generalization about a group of people. They thought Jewish people were not athletic and were too self-centered and selfish to play a team game.

Although these notions about Jewish people were completely false, to succeed in professional baseball, Hank would have to overcome not only those stereotypes but also the prejudice of other players. Many professional baseball players were just like the boys in Hank's old neighborhood and were prejudiced against Jewish people.

The Tigers sent Hank to the minor leagues to begin his professional career. It did not take him very long to realize what life would be like as one of only a few Jewish ballplayers in the game.

Hank was not just the only Jewish player on his team, he was the only Jewish player in the league. Very few of his teammates or opponents had ever met a Jewish person. Few of his teammates talked to him, and he was never invited to go out with them after the game.

One day while Hank was warming up on the field before a game, one of his teammates slowly walked around him, staring. Hank watched him for a minute and then asked, "What are you staring at?"

His teammate looked up. "I have never seen a Jew before," he said. Some people thought all Jewish men had beards, or always wore a special cap called a yarmulke. Some even thought Jewish people had horns!

Hank's teammate shook his head. "I don't understand it. You look just like everybody else."

He should not have been confused, because Hank was just like every other person in the world. While each of us has different talents and abilities, and while we look different from one another, all human beings are essentially the same. And no matter what a person might look like or believe in, our similarities are far more important than our differences. Unfortunately, there were plenty of people who believed otherwise—and still are.

Despite the prejudice he encountered, Hank did well in

the minor leagues, and in 1933 the Tigers brought him to the major leagues.

Although few of Hank's major league teammates had played with a Jewish person before, most of them accepted him, and those who did not knew better than to harass a teammate. While some Detroit fans gave Hank a hard time when he was on the field and called him names, as soon as he stepped into the batter's box, most forgot he was Jewish.

But elsewhere in the league it was different. In some cities, particularly those with small Jewish populations, Hank was viciously taunted by the fans. Hank didn't like it, but he had a thick skin and was determined to succeed.

And succeed he did. After hitting .301 with twelve home runs in his rookie season, he blossomed into stardom in 1934, slugging twenty-six home runs and hitting a robust .339.

Late that season the Tigers were in a race with the New York Yankees for the American League pennant. The Tigers needed to win every game possible.

One day Hank was looking at the team schedule and suddenly realized he had a big problem. On September 10 the Tigers were supposed to play the Boston Red Sox. That was the same day as Rosh Hashanah, the Jewish New Year. In the Jewish religion, Rosh Hashanah is what is known as a high holiday. According to Jewish tradition, Hank, like all Jewish people, was supposed to spend the day reflecting upon his faith. Although Hank wanted to play the game and help his team win, he also wanted to respect his religion. He wasn't sure he should play baseball on such an important day.

As Rosh Hashanah approached, Hank was torn. His teammates and the Tigers fans wanted him to play, but many Jews, including his father, wanted him to skip the game.

A few days before the game, several Detroit sportswriters had an idea. They asked the top rabbi in Detroit whether he thought Hank should play.

The rabbi took the question seriously. He did some research and discovered that in the past, Jewish men had played games on Rosh Hashanah. He also concluded that the Jewish New Year was a joyous occasion that should be enjoyed and celebrated. As far as the rabbi was concerned, it would be fine for Hank to celebrate the game by helping the Tigers beat the Red Sox. He gave Hank approval to play. It probably helped that the rabbi was also a Tigers fan!

The decision was a huge relief to Hank, and when he made his way to the ballpark on Rosh Hashanah, he saw a newsboy in the street holding a stack of newspapers. Hank saw his picture on the cover and decided to take a closer look. As he did, a big smile broke out on his face. Beneath his picture were a few words written in Hebrew, a language used by many Jewish people, and then the same words in English. They read, "Happy New Year!"

Now he could concentrate on baseball. The Tigers needed every win they could get. But Boston played Detroit tough, and entering the seventh inning, the Tigers trailed 1–0.

Then Hank stepped to the plate and dug in against Boston pitcher Gordon Rhodes. He waited for a pitch he liked, then took a hard swing.

The sound of the bat striking the ball echoed through the park and sent the crowd to their feet. The ball rose into the sky in what one sportswriter described as a "towering drive," then cleared the scoreboard for a home run to tie the game 1–1. As he trotted around the bases, Hank was happy, but he also knew his job was not over.

The score was still tied when Hank came to bat in the ninth inning. He let the first pitch pass for a ball. Then the pitcher tried to sneak a fastball over the plate.

Greenberg, according to one sportswriter, "probably never hit a ball as hard as he hit that second pitch." For the second time that day, Hank sent a ball over the scoreboard. As he jogged around the bases, Hank suddenly saw a few fans leap onto the field and run toward him. At first it was only a handful of people, but by the time he rounded third base, there were dozens of fans joining him on his tour of the bases, and hundreds more on the way. When he touched home plate, the joyous crowd collapsed around him. Detroit won 2–1.

Eight days later, with the pennant all but sewn up, Hank had to make another decision. This day was Yom Kippur, the holiest day of the year for Jews. This time, Hank knew what decision to make. Baseball was important, but not as important as Yom Kippur. Instead of going to the game, Hank Greenberg went to the synagogue for religious services.

When he entered the synagogue, he was astounded. The other people attending the service immediately recognized him and began applauding. They appreciated the difficult decision he had made. A few days later, Edgar A. Guest, a popular newspaper columnist, wrote a poem called "Speaking of Greenberg" that ended, "We shall miss him on the infield and shall miss him at the bat / But he's true to his religion—and I honor him for that!"

Unfortunately, although Greenberg was beginning to earn acceptance from players around the league and from fans all over the country, his troubles were not over. The Tigers won the pennant and played in the World Series but lost to the St. Louis Cardinals. Some of the Cardinal players spent much of the series yelling insults at Greenberg, and he hit only one home run.

The next year, 1935, Hank Greenberg became a star. He smacked 36 home runs and knocked in 170 base runners while hitting .328 and leading the Tigers to another pennant.

Hank was eager for another chance to win the World Series. He wondered whether Detroit's opponent, the National League champion Chicago Cubs, would treat him with the respect he deserved as one of the greatest players in baseball.

He got his answer in the first inning of the first game. On only the third pitch of the game, Chicago's leadoff hitter smashed a double. The next Cubs hitter then tapped the ball back to Detroit pitcher Schoolboy Rowe.

As Rowe fielded the ball, Hank raced to first base, placed his foot on the bag, then held out his glove as a target for Rowe. The pitcher swept the ball into his glove, then threw it toward first.

Out of the corner of his eye, Hank saw the Chicago base runner tearing down the baseline, running as fast as he could. That did not concern Hank. His toe was on the edge of the bag, as it should have been, giving the runner plenty of room to tag the base.

But the Cubs had already decided that to beat the Tigers,

they had to beat Greenberg, and decided to treat him as roughly as the Cardinals had the year before. In fact, they decided to treat him even more roughly.

The ball and the base runner reached the bag at almost the same time. But instead of running through the base as usual, the Cubs base runner cut to the inside and ran straight into Greenberg.

Hank took the full brunt of the charge and thudded to the ground. He wasn't hurt badly, but the collision knocked the wind out of him and the ball rolled free. As Hank scrambled to his feet and chased after it, one runner dashed to second base and the other dashed home. The Cubs scored the first run of the game. A few moments later they added another to lead the Tigers 2–0.

In the meantime, the players on the Chicago bench sent a steady stream of insults Greenberg's way. The Cubs were even nastier than the Cardinals had been the year before.

Greenberg tried to ignore them, but after having been knocked to the ground, he didn't play very well the rest of the game. The Tigers lost 3–0.

Even the sportswriters watching the game, many of whom were anti-Semitic themselves, found it hard to believe just how badly the Cubs were behaving. When one reporter asked a Cubs player what words the team was using to taunt Greenberg, he sneered and said, "All of them." One of the umpires, Dolly Stark, was also Jewish, and the Cubs were heckling him with anti-Semitic remarks as well.

Hank was angry, but he was also determined. He wanted to prove to the Cubs that he could not be bullied or intimidated.

In game two the Cubs went out quietly in the top of the first. Then the Tigers came to bat.

The first three Tigers all ripped hits off Cubs pitcher Charlie Root. Hank came up with one man on first and the Tigers already ahead 2–0.

While Tigers fans roared for Greenberg, several Cubs stood at the top of the dugout steps, screaming epithets at him. The big slugger refused to look their way or even to let them know he heard them. It was time for Hank's bat to do his talking.

He didn't hear the crowd and he didn't hear the Cubs players. He focused all his attention on Cubs pitcher Charlie Root.

Root threw a pitch over the plate. Hank swung from his heels, and the crack of the bat against the ball drowned out anything that was being yelled from the Cubs bench.

The ball soared high and deep to left field, over the

scoreboard more than 440 feet from home plate! Greenberg dropped his bat and started his slow jog around the bases.

Home run! Detroit fans cheered wildly.

The Tigers now led 4–0, but that didn't stop the Cubs players. When Hank came up for the second time in the third inning, they were even louder and cruder than before. Umpire George Moriarty was disgusted. A little bench jockeying, or good-natured ribbing, has always been part of the game, but the names they were calling Hank went way over the line.

Moriarty stopped the game, went over to the Cubs bench, and gave the players a piece of his mind. If they didn't stop it, Moriarty told them, he would start throwing players out of the game.

Although that silenced the Cubs, they found other ways to go after Hank. In the seventh inning he came up to bat with a man on and the Tigers leading 7–3. Still angry at the way he had been treated, Hank wanted nothing more than to belt another home run.

The Cubs pitcher, however, had another idea. He wound up and fired the ball.

Hank started to stride toward the pitch, then saw the ball sailing toward his head. In 1935 batters did not yet wear helmets, and a pitch to the head could be deadly.

Without thinking, Greenberg turned away from the pitch and simultaneously raised his arms to block the ball. The pitch struck his wrist flush.

Another player might have jumped in the air and howled out in pain, or run from the batter's box and attacked the pitcher for hitting him on purpose, but Greenberg didn't want to give the Cubs the satisfaction of knowing they had hurt him. He just grimaced and took his base without a word.

After the next Tiger made an out, Pete Fox ripped a hit to the outfield. Teammate Charlie Gehringer scored, and Hank rounded third base determined to follow him across the plate.

Cubs catcher Gabby Hartnett caught the ball and spun to apply the tag.

Hank could have taken out his frustrations by lowering his shoulder and running over Hartnett like a football player, or by sliding with his spikes high and trying to cut him, but even though Hank was still angry, he knew that was not the way to play the game.

Greenberg slid straight at home plate. He and Hartnett collided violently in a cloud of dust.

The umpire hesitated, then raised his right arm. Out! Hank rose slowly and trotted to the Tigers dugout. Even though he had been thrown out, he had shown the Cubs and everyone else how the game was supposed to be played—by the rules.

The Tigers held on to win 8–3 and tie the series at one game apiece. Unfortunately, when Greenberg had slid home, he had broken his wrist. He missed the remainder of the series, but his teammates, inspired by his example, rose to the occasion and beat the Cubs in three of the next four games to take the World Series. Although Greenberg was disappointed at having to sit out, winning a world championship was gratifying.

But it was not as gratifying as standing up to the Cubs. While that was not the last time Hank Greenberg faced taunts on the baseball field, over time many of his opponents and baseball fans began to realize that the only effect those taunts and insults had on Hank was to make him play better. And each day Hank took the field and played the game the right way, he set an example for others. As he did, he helped people understand that although being Jewish made Hank different from most other major leaguers, that difference did not matter, either on the field or off.

Hank went on to play another nine seasons in the major leagues, interrupted by a three-year stint in the Army Air Corps during World War II. In 1935 and 1940 he was named the Most Valuable Player in the American League, and he helped his team win two more pennants and played in two more World Series.

In 1947, his final year in the major leagues, Hank played first base for the Pittsburgh Pirates. That same season, Jackie Robinson of the Brooklyn Dodgers became the first African American to play in the major leagues in the twentieth century.

Like many other players throughout baseball, several of Hank's Pittsburgh teammates were racists, prejudiced against African Americans. Just as Hank had once been taunted for being Jewish, Robinson was taunted for being African American. Some of the Pirates called him terrible names.

Hank was embarrassed by their behavior. The first time Jackie reached first base against the Pirates, Greenberg realized that he and Robinson had an awful lot in common. As Greenberg later recalled, "He got a hit and stood beside me on first base with his chin up, like a prince. I had a feeling for him, because of the way I had been treated."

Hank turned to Jackie and said simply, "Don't let them get you down. You are doing fine. Keep it up."

That is the lesson of Hank Greenberg, and that is exactly what Jackie Robinson would do.

JACKIE'S BIG TEST

IN AUGUST OF 1883 the Chicago White Stockings of the National League traveled to Ohio to play an exhibition game against a minor league team, the Toledo Blue Stockings. At the time the White Stockings, led by their captain Cap Anson, were one of the best teams in professional baseball, winners of the pennant each of the previous three seasons.

Thousands of Toledo baseball fans came out for the game. They were excited about the opportunity to see the great White Stockings play.

About a half hour before the game was scheduled to begin, both teams took the field, the White Stockings on one side and the Blue Stockings on the other. Players paired up and began tossing the ball back and forth.

After only a few moments the catcher for the Blue Stockings approached his manager, Charles Morton.

"I don't think I can play today," he said. "My hand is so sore I can hardly stand to catch the ball." In the 1880s catchers did not wear gloves, and hand injuries were common.

Morton was disappointed. His catcher was no scrub. The graduate of Oberlin College had a terrific arm; Toledo's star pitcher, Tony Mullane, later called him "the best catcher I ever worked with." Still, Morton gave the young man the day off and told Toledo's second-string catcher to get ready for the game.

On the other side of the field, White Stockings captain Cap Anson was playing catch with a teammate. Suddenly, he stopped and stared over at a player in a Toledo uniform standing off to the side. Anson was shocked. The player was African American.

It was the injured catcher, Moses Fleetwood Walker.

Anson raced over to Toledo manager Charles Morton and started sputtering in protest. Anson, like many other Americans at the time, was a racist, and thought black people were not as good as white people. He told Morton that the White Stockings would never, ever share the field with a black person. Then Anson turned to Walker and ordered him off the field.

Walker stood his ground and looked at Morton without saying a word.

Morton tried to calm Anson down. He wasn't completely surprised at the Chicago captain's reaction. Walker was one of only a handful of African Americans playing professional baseball. On several other occasions Toledo's opponents had expressed surprise at seeing Walker behind the plate. Some had complained and even called Walker crude names, but no team had refused to play the Blue Stockings.

Morton told Anson that he expected the White Stockings to fulfill their contract and play the game. After all, he explained, Walker was hurt and wasn't even going to play. All he would do was sit on the Toledo bench and support his teammates.

That wasn't good enough for Anson. He argued and tried to bully the Toledo manager, but Morton refused to back down. In fact, Morton told Anson, on second thought, Walker *was* playing. He inserted the player into the Toledo lineup in the outfield, where it was unlikely that he would have to catch more than a ball or two with his sore hand. Morton then told Anson that if the White Stockings refused to play, they would not receive their share of the ticket money for the game.

This made Anson and the other White Stockings even angrier, but they did not want to lose their money. As he walked away, Anson turned back to Morton and said, "We won't never play no more with any niggers on the field." The game then went on without incident, the White Stockings winning 7–6. Moses Walker went hitless.

Word of Anson's outburst traveled fast, and sadly, virtually everyone in the National League, from the players to the men who owned the teams, agreed with Anson. The following season when the Toledo club joined the American Association, which at the time was also considered a major league, several other teams let the Toledo manager know that if Walker played, Toledo would no longer be welcome in the league.

In midseason Walker was hurt, and at the end of the season Toledo released the young player from his contract. The following season no major league team signed Walker or any other African American ballplayer to a contract. The men who ran major league baseball decided among themselves that African Americans would not be allowed to play organized baseball. This decision established the "color line," the separation of black and white races that existed in almost every area of American society. Although no rule was ever put in writing, for the next sixty-three years no one tested the color line in major league baseball.

Then came Jackie Robinson.

When Jackie Robinson was growing up in Pasadena, California, just outside Los Angeles, he had never heard of Moses Fleetwood Walker. In Pasadena, children of all races played and went to school together. Jackie had been born in Georgia in 1919, but shortly after he was born, his father, Jerry, left the family, leaving Jackie's mother to take care of him and his three older brothers and older sister. Jackie's mother then moved the family to Pasadena to be near her brother, and she got a job as a maid.

Because his mother worked so much, Jackie was often left on his own after school. He tagged along with his older brothers, playing football and baseball and basketball, and games like tag in the streets. As he grew older, he fell in with a group his own age that included boys of African American, white, Mexican, and Japanese heritage. They called themselves the Pepper Street Gang. Although the group occasionally got into trouble with the local police, the Pepper Street Gang was nothing like the gangs that plague so many cities and towns today. Jackie and the other members of the gang liked to compete, and they challenged other groups of boys all around Los Angeles to games of baseball, football, and other sports.

All the Robinson children were fine athletes. In junior high Jackie played football, baseball, and basketball and ran track, and even won a citywide tournament in Ping-Pong. Some of his white friends dreamed about playing major league baseball, but by the time he was a teenager, Jackie knew that would be impossible for him. Even though there were all-black professional baseball teams, Jackie understood that for most African American young men, there were few opportunities to play sports professionally as an adult. Whenever anyone asked Jackie what he wanted to be when he grew up, he told them he wanted to be a coach.

Jackie's older brother Mack was a big track star in high school. He went on to compete for Pasadena Junior College and earned a scholarship to the University of Oregon, where he became one of the best sprinters in the country. In 1936 Mack made the U.S. Olympic team and won a silver medal at the games in Germany.

After high school Jackie followed Mack's footsteps to Pasadena Junior College for his freshman and sophomore years; he then went to the University of California at Los

Angeles, or UCLA. Jackie was a terrific all-around athlete, and in his first year at UCLA, his junior year, he competed in track, football, basketball, and baseball. He played short-stop on the baseball team, and once he got on base, he was almost impossible to throw out. He drove the opposition crazy stealing bases.

Despite his accomplishments, when Jackie looked to the future, he did not like what he saw. Despite having won a silver medal and having earned a college degree, Jackie's brother Mack had a hard time finding work simply because of the color of his skin. And Jackie worried about the sacrifices his family was making to help him attend college. In the spring of his senior year he dropped out, later writing, "I was convinced that no amount of education would help a black man get a job . . . I could see no future in staying at college, no real future in athletics."

After working briefly at a youth camp, Jackie played semipro football, baseball, and softball on the West Coast, earning barely enough money to help support his aging mother. Then, on April 3, 1941, Jackie was drafted into the army.

Stationed at an army base in Kansas, Jackie, a natural leader, was one of only a few African American soldiers at the time to become an officer. In the spring of 1943 he tried to join the camp baseball team, a squad that included several major league players. Jackie had seen them practice and knew he was good enough to play, but he was told the team was for white soldiers only. If he wanted to play baseball, he would have to play on the black team.

Jackie knew that wasn't right, and he complained. As a result he was transferred to another base in Fort Hood, Texas. This time he didn't try to join the base team. Instead, soon after he arrived, he started his own battalion baseball team for black players.

On July 6, 1944, Jackie Robinson's life changed. The army base was very big, and soldiers and other workers there often took buses to get around. The buses, like many other kinds of public transportation in the United States at the time, were segregated. That meant whites and African Americans were kept apart from one another. Segregation was common, particularly in the South, where it was the law. In many places, African Americans and whites used different drinking fountains and restrooms, attended different schools, ate in separate restaurants, and sat apart at sporting events.

On July 6, Jackie, wearing his officer's uniform, boarded the bus at Camp Hood. When he stepped aboard, he saw that most of the seats in the very back, where African Americans were supposed to sit, were occupied, as were most of the seats in the front, which were occupied by white soldiers and staff. But near the middle of the bus he found an empty seat next to a woman. Jackie recognized her as African American, but she had very light skin. Jackie sat down.

The bus didn't move. From his seat in front, the bus driver glared at Jackie in the rearview mirror. He thought Jackie was sitting next to a white woman. "Move to the back!" he called out.

Jackie was confused. He looked around, wondering who the bus driver was talking to. Then he heard the voice again. "I mean you! Move to the back or I'll make trouble for you when we get to the bus station!"

The bus turned silent as all the passengers watched the confrontation. Jackie didn't move. He knew he had every right to sit wherever he wanted. "That's up to you," Jackie answered as he sat in the seat, his eyes blazing.

The bus driver tried once more. "Move back or get off the bus!" he yelled. But Jackie stayed put. He rode the bus in silence until it arrived at the bus station. Then the driver, true to his word, reported Robinson's behavior, and Jackie was arrested by military police.

Although Jackie was court-martialed, he was acquitted. Later that fall he was honorably discharged from the army.

The incident had a big impact on Jackie's future. African American newspapers all over the country reported the story, and Jackie, who was already well known as an athlete, became a hero to many African Americans for refusing to move from his seat and for standing up against segregation.

But the incident also left Jackie without a job.

Jackie found work as a basketball coach at a small college that winter, and in the spring he wrote to the Kansas City Monarchs of the Negro Leagues and asked for a tryout. Jackie wanted to get married to his girlfriend, Rachel, and to do that he needed a job. Playing Negro League baseball was his best opportunity to earn a living.

After being banned from playing professional baseball with whites, African Americans had started their own teams, which played in what were known as the Negro Leagues. Although the Negro Leagues were not as well organized as the all-white major leagues, their teams and players were just as good as their major league counterparts, if not better. A black catcher named Josh Gibson was known as "the black Babe Ruth," and became famous for his long home runs. Many people believed that Negro League pitcher Satchel Paige was the best pitcher in the history of the game, and "Cool Papa" Bell was such a fast base runner, his fans joked that he could turn out a light switch in his bedroom and be under the covers before it got dark. Negro League teams traveled the country, and thousands of fans, both black and white, turned out to watch them play. Although all the travel made life tough in the Negro Leagues, at a time when the average American made only $50 a week, most Negro League players made twice that amount, and the best players, like Paige, were wealthy.

The Kansas City Monarchs had once been one of the best teams in the Negro Leagues. After a poor season in 1944, they were beginning to rebuild. Even though Jackie was a little rusty, he made the team during spring training and in 1945 signed a contract for $400 a month.

Jackie's contract was big news in African American newspapers all over the country. Even though he had yet to play an official game in the Negro Leagues, some African American sportswriters were already thinking that if an African American were ever to play in the major leagues, Jackie Robinson might be that man. He was more than a talented athlete. He had grown up around all kinds of people, had attended college, and was a military veteran. With his background, Jackie Robinson would be the perfect candidate to break the color line in the big leagues. There were good people all over the country, white and black, who were trying to remove the barrier. After all, thousands of African Americans had served their country during World War II. If a man could risk his life in the defense of his country, these people asked, why could he not play in the major leagues?

One of those people, Isadore Muchnick, was a city councilman in Boston. Each season the Boston Red Sox needed approval from the city council to play baseball on Sundays. Muchnick thought African American players deserved an opportunity to play in the major leagues and threatened to withhold approval for Sunday baseball unless the Red Sox held a tryout for African American players. The Red Sox reluctantly agreed.

Despite his having played only a few games in the Negro Leagues, Jackie and two other Negro Leaguers, Sam Jethroe and Marvin Williams, were invited to try out for the Boston Red Sox.

On a cool, gray morning on April 16, 1945, the three men arrived at Fenway Park. After changing into their Negro League uniforms, they stepped onto the field, where

Red Sox coach Hugh Duffy was conducting a tryout for several dozen white players.

Jackie looked up at the towering left-field wall, known today as the "Green Monster." It seemed so close, he could almost touch it, but so high, he could hardly imagine hitting a ball over it. The three players warmed up a bit, fielded some ground balls, shagged some flies hit by Duffy, and then were invited to take batting practice.

Jackie was determined to do his best. Even though he did not believe the Red Sox were sincere in offering the tryout, Jackie wanted to prove that he belonged.

He stood in the batter's box and felt the same butterflies in his stomach he felt before any big game. Then he spat on his hands, rubbed them together, got a good grip on the bat, and dug his feet into the batter's box. He was ready. The batting-practice pitcher wound up and threw the ball Jackie's way.

The butterflies disappeared as Jackie started his swing.

Crack! He hit the pitch on the fat part of the bat and sent a line drive toward the wall.

Whump! The ball rocketed off the wall and back toward the infield. Another pitch delivered another *Crack!* and the next another loud *Whump!* Jackie lined pitch after pitch off the wall, or hard down the left-field line, or deep into the outfield. With each swing Jackie was passing the test and proving that African Americans were good enough to play in the major leagues.

And then there was a voice yelling in anger from far up in the grandstand, so far up in the shadows that it was impossible to tell exactly who was hollering. But it was easy to hear what was said.

"Get those niggers off the field!" The words echoed through the ballpark as loudly as any crack off the bat.

The tryout was suddenly over. Robinson, Jethroe, and Williams were told to go home. They quickly changed into their street clothes and left the ballpark. Days later the Red Sox announced that they wouldn't sign any of the Negro League players to a contract. Jackie Robinson was not surprised. He did not believe any African American would play in the major leagues anytime soon.

Jackie returned to the Monarchs and played well, earning a spot on the Negro League all-star team. Two weeks later Jackie was surprised when he was told that Branch Rickey, the president and owner of the Brooklyn Dodgers of the major leagues, wanted to meet with him. Jackie didn't know it, but one of Rickey's scouts, Clyde Sukeforth, had been quietly scouting Jackie for months, and Rickey had been looking into Jackie's background. Rickey knew that Jackie was more than a good ballplayer. He was also a special person. And Branch Rickey needed a special person.

When Jackie arrived at Rickey's office in Brooklyn, he assumed that Rickey wanted to talk to him about playing for the Brooklyn Brown Bombers, a new Negro League team Rickey was rumored to be putting together.

Rickey interviewed Jackie, asking him about his family and getting to know him. Then he revealed the reason he had asked Jackie to meet. He told Robinson that he wanted to sign him to a contract to play for the Dodgers—not the Brown Dodgers, but the major league Dodgers, the Brooklyn Dodgers of the National League! He thought Jackie could be the first African American to play in the major leagues since Moses Fleetwood Walker. Jackie was stunned.

Rickey explained to him that it was not going to be easy to make it to the major leagues. Not only was the competition tough, but Jackie was certain to face prejudice from fans and players and be the target of all sorts of racial insults. But no matter what happened, explained Rickey, Jackie could not show his anger. If he failed, either as a player or as a person, narrow-minded people who believed African Americans should not or could not play major league baseball would point to Robinson as proof.

Rickey wanted to make sure Jackie knew just how much was at stake and told him that if he failed, it might be years before another African American was given a chance to play in the major leagues, and the cause of equal rights for African Americans could be set back. No matter what happened, Rickey told Robinson, even if he was struck by another player and challenged to a fight, he would have to keep his cool.

Jackie was puzzled. "Mr. Rickey," he asked, "what do you want? Do you want a ballplayer who is afraid to fight back?"

Rickey paused and looked Jackie in the eye. "I want a ballplayer with the guts enough not to fight back," he said.

Jackie understood.

Then, to make sure Jackie understood, Rickey took off his coat, came out from behind his desk, and got in Jackie's face. He acted out several situations that Jackie was certain to face, pretending he was a hotel clerk and refusing Jackie a room, and mimicking a fan heckling Jackie on the street. Then Rickey pretended he was a base runner who had just slid into Jackie and been tagged out. "So I jump up," yelled Rickey, "and I yell, 'Don't hit me with the ball like that, you tar baby!' So I haul off and sock you right in the cheek." His voice booming and his fist cocked in the air, Rickey then yelled, "What do you do now, Jackie? What do you do now?"

Jackie paused, and even though he could feel his blood pressure rising, he took a deep breath. "I get it, Mr. Rickey," he said. "I've got another cheek."

That was just the answer Rickey wanted. Jackie had passed the first test. Rickey offered Jackie a contract for the 1946 season, and Jackie carefully signed it.

Jackie was on his way to the major leagues. Yet even though he had promised Branch Rickey that no matter what happened he would turn the other cheek, Jackie was not sure he could keep that promise. He knew a time would come when he would be tested.

Rickey kept the signing a secret until the end of the season. Then, on October 23, 1945, one of the Dodgers' minor league teams, the Montreal Royals of the International League, made the announcement that Robinson had signed a contract with the Dodgers and would play with Montreal in the 1946 season. If Robinson proved himself in Montreal, the Dodgers would bring him up to the major leagues.

That was front-page news all over the country. African American fans in particular were thrilled. They knew that if Jackie made it in the major leagues, he would help prove to prejudiced people that African Americans were just as good as everyone else and should be allowed to do any job they were qualified to do. If baseball became integrated, it would help prove that blacks and whites could get along and that segregation was not necessary. Someday, African Americans would no longer have to use separate restrooms, attend different schools, or sit at the back of the bus. Jackie could help change everything.

When Jackie arrived in Florida for spring training with the Royals, he wasn't sure what to expect. Many of his teammates had never really known an African American before, and while they were not mean to Jackie, they were not very friendly, either. Some fans in Florida were less kind. Segregation was the law in Florida. The Royals actually had to move their training camp from one city to another after residents complained, and during spring training games black fans who came to cheer Jackie still had to sit in a special section of the stands. Jackie got off to a slow start, but by the end of camp he had earned a job as the team's second baseman. He was playing well, but he knew that the real test would come during the regular season.

The Royals opened the season in Jersey City, New Jersey. More than twenty-five thousand fans, black and white, crammed into the ballpark. Some supported Jackie, and others were just curious, but everyone knew they were about to witness history.

When Jackie came to bat for the first time, the crowd buzzed. They didn't quite know what to make of him. Some had never seen a black person play baseball.

Jackie had never been more nervous in his life. Would the pitcher throw at his head? Would the umpires treat him fairly? Would the fans boo him or call him names?

He just tried to focus on the pitcher. He got a good pitch to hit but was too anxious and hit an easy ground ball to shortstop. Jackie was out, but with his first at-bat out of the way, he began to relax. He had been treated like any other player.

When he came to bat the next time, there were two runners on base. This time, Jackie wasn't thinking about what might happen. He was just thinking of trying to help his team win.

The pitcher wound up and threw the ball toward the plate. The pitch was exactly where Jackie liked it, over the middle of the plate and just above his waist. He lashed out at the ball with his bat.

The ball took off on a line toward left field. All twenty-five thousand fans stood at the same time and watched the ball streak to left. Jackie tore out of the batter's box and sprinted toward first base.

The Jersey City left fielder turned and ran back, but as he approached the fence he slowed down, then stopped, looking up. The ball sailed over his head and over the fence for a home run!

Jackie saw the umpire signal home run and heard the roar of the crowd. He barely felt his feet touch the ground as he ran the bases. When he rounded third base, his manager, Clay Hopper, who was coaching third, patted him on the back, just as he would have done to any other player. As Jackie ran home, he saw the next hitter, his teammate George Shuba, standing near home plate. Many in the ballpark wondered how Shuba would greet Jackie. Would he treat him like any other teammate, or would he ignore him because of the color of his skin?

As Jackie crossed home plate and headed toward the dugout, Shuba answered that question. Shuba reached out his hand toward Jackie and Jackie reached out his hand to Shuba. The two men shook hands, and for the first time in more than sixty years, a white ballplayer congratulated his African American teammate. When Jackie reached the dugout, the rest of the Royals swarmed around him.

But Jackie wasn't done. The Royals went on to win 14–1,

and Jackie finished with four hits, four runs batted in, four runs scored, and two stolen bases. He wasn't just good, he was the best player on the field! Montreal sportswriter Baz O'Meara called his performance "another Emancipation Day for the Negro race."

That was just the beginning. For the rest of the season Jackie ran wild for the Royals, knocking out base hits, driving pitchers nuts with his daring base running, and leading the team to the league championship. Montreal fans loved him and treated him well. Elsewhere in the league, however, just as Branch Rickey had predicted, Jackie was not so easily accepted. In some cities he was not allowed to stay in the same hotel as his teammates. Some fans cruelly heckled him, as did many opposing players, trying to make him so miserable that he would quit baseball forever. Pitchers sometimes threw at his head, and just as Rickey had cautioned, base runners slid into Jackie hard, their spikes held high, calling him names and challenging him to fight.

But they could not beat Jackie or make him quit. Never, not even once, did Jackie lose his cool, keeping his word to Rickey. He turned the other cheek, hoping for a chance to play for the Dodgers. He knew that playing in the major leagues would be the real test, both of his ability as a ballplayer and of his character.

Branch Rickey was determined to give Jackie that chance after the 1946 season, but he knew that the other baseball owners were against him. They didn't want Jackie or any other African American player to appear in the major leagues. In January of 1946 they all met in New York and held a cowardly secret vote. Although the other owners were against Jackie, they were afraid to say so in public. Every team owner in the major league except Rickey voted to keep Jackie out of baseball.

Branch Rickey was angry. A few days after the meeting he went to see the commissioner of baseball, Happy Chandler. If Chandler approved Jackie's contract, then Jackie could play in the major leagues, no matter how the other owners felt.

When Rickey asked Chandler if he would approve the contract, the commissioner responded, "I'm going to have to meet my maker someday, and if he asks me why I didn't let this boy play and I say it's because he's black, that might not be a satisfactory answer. So bring him in."

That was all Rickey needed to hear. The following spring, in 1947, Branch Rickey invited Jackie to spring training with the Dodgers. If Jackie played well, Rickey intended to bring him to the major leagues.

Once again Jackie had a tough time in the spring. The Dodgers asked him to play a new position, first base. Due to segregation he had to live and eat separately from his teammates. A few Dodgers told Rickey they would not play with an African American and asked to be traded. Others acted as if Jackie were invisible. It was tough for him to concentrate on baseball under such conditions. But as the regular season approached, he played better and better, and earned a place in the starting lineup as the Dodger first baseman. At the end of spring training Branch Rickey released a statement that read, "The Brooklyn Dodgers today purchased the contract of Jackie Roosevelt Robinson from the Montreal Royals. He will report immediately." It was official. Jackie was going to be a major leaguer. Every game would be a test.

The Dodgers opened the regular season on April 15 in Brooklyn against the Boston Braves. Jackie got off to a quiet start and went hitless. In the Dodgers' second game he got his first hit, a bunt single, and in the next two games he started to relax and hit a home run and several other hits.

To this point, although Jackie wasn't exactly welcomed by his opponents, he had not been treated badly. They basically ignored him, and the Brooklyn fans were supportive.

Then the Philadelphia Phillies came to town.

Phillies manager Ben Chapman disliked African Americans and was not ashamed to say so. Although like many Americans his attitude later changed, in 1947 he hated the idea that a black man was playing in the major leagues. He ordered his team to see if Robinson could "take it."

During the Dodgers' sweep of the three-game series, the Phillies played as if they didn't care whether they won or lost. All they cared about was harassing Jackie.

Every time Jackie stepped up to the plate, the Phillies players gathered at the top of the dugout steps and screamed profanities at him. Led by Chapman, they called Jackie every name they could think of.

Inside, Jackie had never been so angry in his life, not even when he had been ordered to the back of the bus at Fort Hood. Every instinct in his body told him to walk off the field and go home, or else to go over to the dugout and challenge the Phillies players to a fight.

But Jackie knew he could not do this. In fact, he could not even let the Phillies know he heard them. But of course, he did hear them. There was only a small crowd in the ballpark, and Jackie heard every word. He later recalled that it seemed as if the name-calling "had been synchronized by some master conductor." Many of his teammates were appalled. One, Howie Schultz, later said of the abuse, "If you said those things today, you'd start another Civil War."

But Jackie ignored the taunts. Each time he came to bat, he tried to imagine a day in the future when there would be other African Americans in the big leagues and reminded himself that he had to stand and take it for their sake. He just stared straight ahead at the pitcher and tried to concentrate on getting a hit.

The Phillies were not going to make that easy. Chapman ordered his pitchers to throw at Jackie. If they refused, he told them he would fine them.

Jackie never knew whether the pitcher would throw a strike or throw at him. Each time a pitch whistled toward his head, he spun out of the way. Sometimes he even fell to the ground to avoid the pitch. Each time he did, he simply dusted off his uniform and stepped back into the batter's box, more determined than ever.

Jackie had to be just as careful when he was playing the field. Every time a Phillies batter raced to first base, Jackie had to catch the ball, then get out of the way fast. He knew that if the Phillies had the opportunity, they would run him down.

For three long days the Phillies did everything they could to see if Jackie could take it. And each time he ignored their harassment, Jackie proved that he was not only the better player but also the better person. Even some Dodgers who still were not sure they liked having an African American teammate were offended by the way the Phillies treated Jackie. In the last game, one of Jackie's teammates, Eddie Stanky, had enough. Between innings he angrily approached several Philadelphia players and told them to "pick on somebody who can fight back." Game by game, little by little, Jackie was earning the respect of everyone who saw him play.

That didn't stop the Phillies or some other teams from continuing to test Jackie, but to his teammates, and to himself, Jackie had already passed the biggest test he would face. He had proven that he could take it. And as the season went on, Jackie proved that he was one of the best players in the league, a fine hitter and an exciting base runner who was a threat to steal every time he got on base.

Later that season, on July 3, the Cleveland Indians signed African American outfielder Larry Doby to a contract and he made his debut two days later. Jackie was not alone in the major leagues.

There would be no turning back. Over time every team in baseball would put an African American on the field, and today no one thinks twice about seeing a player of any race or nationality either on the baseball field or in the workplace. By breaking the color line, Jackie did not just win the right for African Americans to play in the major leagues, he also reminded the entire country that people should be judged only by their abilities and their character.

He also proved that he was a far better person than those who tried to see if he could take it. Jackie went on to lead the Dodgers to the pennant in 1947 and was named the National League Rookie of the Year, an award that today is known as the Jackie Robinson Award. For the next decade he was one of the greatest players in the history of the game, and in 1962 he became the first African American to be inducted into the National Baseball Hall of Fame. Today there are African Americans in every professional sport, and segregation no longer exists in America.

In every way possible, Jackie Robinson passed the test.

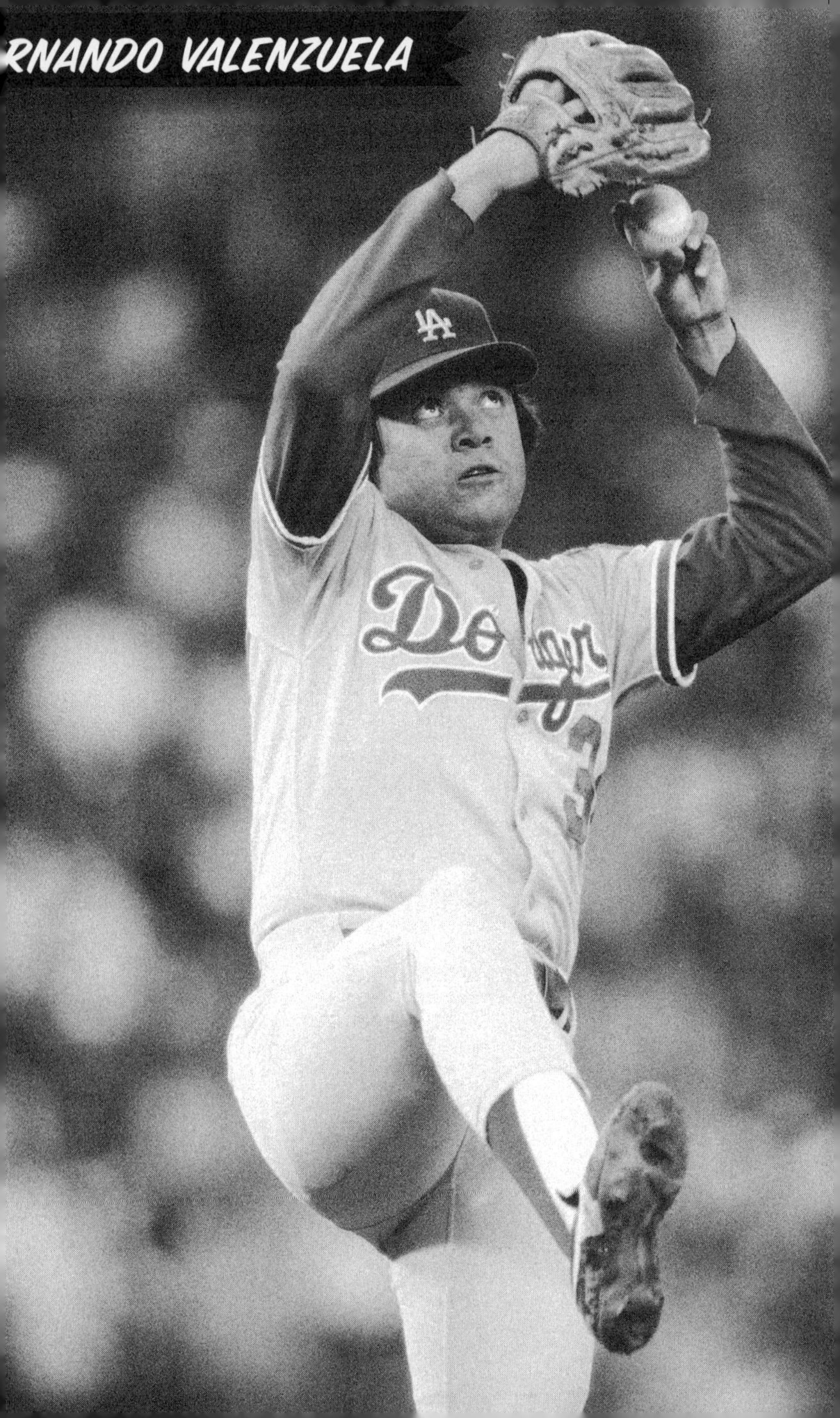
RNANDO VALENZUELA

FERNANDOMANIA

ON OPENING DAY OF THE 1981 BASEBALL SEASON, Los Angeles Dodgers manager Tommy Lasorda sat in his office thinking. One day earlier he had learned that Jerry Reuss, his first choice to start the game, had pulled a muscle in his leg and could not pitch. His next choice, pitcher Burt Hooten, had a sore toe and would not be ready for another day.

Lasorda looked at his roster and shook his head. None of his other veteran starting pitchers had enough rest. Who would pitch for the Dodgers on opening day?

As the manager considered his options, he kept coming to the same conclusion. The only pitcher who might be available to start was Fernando Valenzuela.

Lasorda thought Fernando was a fine pitcher with a

good future, but the young native of Mexico was still a rookie. He had only pitched a few innings in relief in the major leagues at the very end of the previous season and was still very inexperienced. Only twenty years old, he was one of the youngest players in the major leagues. Lasorda hoped to bring him along slowly. The Dodgers' opponents on opening day were the Houston Astros, the defending champions of the National League's Western Division. Although Fernando had pitched well in spring training, he had pitched batting practice the previous day. The Dodgers manager wasn't even sure that Fernando would have the strength to pitch on two consecutive days. Still, Lasorda had no other choice.

He went to Fernando's locker and placed a brand-new baseball in his glove. That is sometimes the way a baseball manager lets a player know he is the starting pitcher. Lasorda hoped he was not making a mistake. He had told Fernando the day before that he might start, but now it was official. He hoped that Fernando could just pitch long enough and well enough to give the Dodgers a chance to win.

When Fernando arrived at Dodger Stadium and looked in his glove, he found the brand-new baseball. He now knew for certain that he was going to be the starting pitcher. Another pitcher might have become nervous or gotten excited, but even though he was pleased the expression on Fernando's face did not change. He was confident and ready.

A few hours later Fernando was warming up in the bullpen. More than fifty thousand fans filled the stands. Only the most dedicated Dodger rooters had heard of Fernando Valenzuela before or even remembered that he had pitched at the end of the previous season. And when he took the mound to start the game and began throwing his final warm-up pitches, some fans, in fact, even started to laugh. Fernando did not look like he was twenty years old. He looked closer to forty. He was short, a little pudgy, with a mop of dark hair that sat on top of his head like a wig, and his uniform didn't seem to fit very well. He looked more as if he should be up in the stands eating popcorn than down on the pitcher's mound.

When he wound up to throw the ball, he looked even less like a pitcher. As he lifted his leg in his wind-up and raised his arms above his head, he spun around, almost turning his back on the batter. Instead of looking at his catcher's target, he tilted his head back and looked straight up in the air before spinning back around, catching sight of his target, and firing the ball home.

Even though the stands were full and the box seats

were occupied by some of the biggest stars in Hollywood, Fernando did not look nervous. In fact, he always looked a little tired, even bored. But as the Houston Astros and every baseball fan in America would soon learn, not only did Fernando look like no other pitcher in game, he threw like no other pitcher in the game.

Astros All-Star outfielder Terry Puhl led off the game, but Fernando pitched as if he were the All-Star and Puhl were the rookie, getting him out on an easy ground ball. Although the next batter singled, Fernando easily retired Houston's two best hitters, César Cedeño and José Cruz.

For the next eight innings, spinning and looking to the heavens before each pitch, he mowed down the defending National League Western Division champions as if they were a bunch of Little Leaguers. With each out, the Dodger Stadium crowd came alive. By the end of the game they were cheering every pitch.

When the last hitter, Dave Roberts, stepped up to bat, the Dodgers were leading 2–0 and the crowd was on their feet, chanting, "Fernando, Fernando, Fernando," over and over again. Fernando got two strikes on the hitter and then, for the 105th time in the game, he wound up, spun away from the hitter, stretched his arms over his head, looked to the sky, then whirled and threw the ball toward home.

Whiff! Roberts lunged at the ball and missed it, and the umpire's arm shot into the air. Strike three! Fernando had not just won the game, he had thrown a shutout in his very first start, on opening day, in front of thousands of people! In an instant, almost everyone in southern California knew his name. "Who is this Fernando Valenzuela," they wondered, "and where does he come from and how did he get here?"

Fernandomania was about to begin.

After the Brooklyn Dodgers signed Jackie Robinson and brought him to the major leagues in 1947, integrating major league baseball, the Dodgers went on to sign many other African American players. They developed a reputation as one of the most progressive franchises in baseball.

After the 1957 season the Dodgers moved from Brooklyn to Los Angeles. At first they played in the Los Angeles Coliseum, a gigantic stadium that was usually used for football. But in 1960 the Dodgers broke ground on their own ballpark, Dodger Stadium.

The site for the ballpark, just outside downtown Los Angeles, was known as Chavez Ravine. It was the home of a small community of Mexican immigrants, a tightly knit group of people who had created their own neighborhood in the shadows of downtown Los Angeles, a safe place where they lived much the same way many of them had in Mexico. All their children played together, and most families still had small gardens where they grew their favorite foods. Some even kept chickens and goats.

Baseball is very popular in Mexico, and many of the residents of Chavez Ravine were happy when they learned that the Dodgers were moving to Los Angeles. But when they learned that the city had given the Dodgers permission to build a new ballpark in Chavez Ravine, those smiles turned to frowns. Although each resident who owned his or her property would be paid for it, everyone in the neighborhood would have to move.

The residents of Chavez Ravine tried to fight the decision in court, but they were unable to stop the city from allowing the Dodgers to build their new ballpark. Bulldozers knocked down their homes, and the residents of Chavez Ravine scattered to other Los Angeles neighborhoods.

The Mexican community in southern California felt that they had been mistreated and discriminated against because of their heritage. Even though many Mexicans Americans were baseball fans, very, very few became fans of the Los Angeles Dodgers.

Historically, professional baseball had not treated players from Mexico and other Latin American countries quite as badly as they had treated African Americans, but Latinos had not exactly been welcomed, either. Light-skinned Latino players were allowed to play in the United States, and in the first half of the twentieth century a handful of players from Cuba, Puerto Rico, and other Latin American countries and Caribbean Islands played in the major leagues.

The first Mexican player to reach the major leagues was Mel Almada, an outfielder for the Boston Red Sox, in 1933. But players from Latin America were rare, and any Latin American ballplayer of African ancestry was banned from the major leagues entirely.

After Jackie Robinson broke the color line in 1947, that began to change, and by the late 1950s and 1960s Latin Americans became more common in the major leagues. A handful, like the great outfielder Roberto Clemente of the Pittsburgh Pirates, who became the first Latino named to the Baseball Hall of Fame, became big stars.

But most Latino players still had a difficult time. Most did not know how to speak English, which made it difficult for them in professional baseball. Few teammates or coaches spoke Spanish, either, so even the simple things, like ordering food in a restaurant or buying clothes, were challenging. Many of these men faced segregation for the first time in their lives and did not understand why they were prevented from eating and living where they wanted to. Many talented players became homesick and simply gave up and returned to their native land before ever reaching the major leagues.

Those who did reach the majors were not always treated well. Some Americans assumed that all Latin Americans were the same, when in reality people from different Latin American cultures enjoy different foods and music, just as Americans of different backgrounds or regions do. Many fans and baseball officials believed in stereotypes that simply were not true, and thought Latin American players were lazy or hot tempered. As a result, these players were often misunderstood, and it was difficult for them to feel comfortable living and playing baseball in America.

Mexico shares a long border with the United States, and Mexican Americans make up the largest Latino group in the United States. Yet although baseball is very popular in Mexico, even after Jackie Robinson broke the color line, very few Mexican players reached the major leagues. By 1980 only a few dozen had played in the majors. None had become a big star, and no major league team really reached out to Mexican and Mexican American fans.

Although millions of people in southern California were of Mexican heritage, and Los Angeles was founded by Spanish immigrants from what is now Mexico, not even the Los Angeles Dodgers tried to attract Mexican American fans. In fact, by 1980, in the entire history of the Dodgers franchise, only one Mexican player, José Peña, a pitcher who played for the Dodgers in parts of three seasons from 1970 to 1972, had ever worn a Dodgers uniform.

Today, however, thousands of Mexican American and other Latinos turn out for games at Dodger Stadium and other major league ballparks. Most major league games are now broadcast in both English and Spanish, and Latino fans have embraced baseball in the United States just as they have done in their native lands.

One big reason for that is that pudgy young pitcher from Mexico, Fernando Valenzuela. He may have saved our national pastime.

After Fernando's opening day victory, the press crowded around him in the locker room, peppering him with questions in English that he did not understand. Mike Brito, the Dodgers scout who had signed Fernando, was a native of Cuba. He spoke Spanish and translated for the young rookie.

Fernando Valenzuela answered the questions as if he had held a press conference every day of his life. When a reporter asked if he was afraid to pitch in front of fifty thousand fans, Fernando smiled and said, "I didn't mind the fifty thousand fans as much as I mind these two dozen newspaper reporters."

And when another reporter asked if he was afraid, Fernando looked at him with a puzzled expression on his face. "When I get on the mound," he said, "I do not know what afraid is."

That was because even though Fernando was only twenty years old, he had already spent much of his life playing baseball. Over these many years, he had worked very hard, perfecting the natural abilities he had for the game.

Fernando was born in 1960 nearly seven hundred miles south of Los Angeles, and two hundred miles south of the U.S. border, in Etchohuaquila, a small farm town near Mexico's west coast. The village had no plumbing and the streets were dirt and gravel. He was the youngest of twelve children. As a boy Fernando played soccer and baseball with his brothers and cousins. Baseball was his favorite sport. After everyone finished working in the fields, they usually played a game. When Fernando was thirteen years old, he was allowed to play with the other adults, and played first base on his town team. He was one of eighteen Valenzuelas—and the youngest—on the team.

Fernando never dreamed of playing in the major leagues. He just hoped to be the best Valenzuela. Fernando's older brother Rafael, however, saw something special in his baby brother, calling him a natural, and encouraged him to start pitching. Fernando took the mound for several local amateur teams and at age fifteen was offered $80 a month to turn professional and play for a team in the nearby city of Navajoa. He quit school and accepted the contract.

Over the next few years he played baseball morning, noon, and night, appearing in hundreds of games and pitching hundreds of innings, learning a little more each time.

There were several professional leagues in Mexico at the time, and at age seventeen Fernando worked his way up to the biggest one, the Mexican League, which is still considered to be equal in strength to the best American minor leagues.

He was pitching for Puebla when Dodgers scout Mike Brito saw him for the first time. Brito was at the game to scout another player, a shortstop, when he noticed that the pitcher for the opposing team was striking out a lot of hitters. Brito forgot about the shortstop and began watching the pitcher more closely. He noticed that the pitcher had a good, moving fastball, a good sharp-breaking curveball, and a quick slider. He looked as though he had been pitching his whole life, and had great control.

Brito looked at the man on the mound and at first assumed that he was too old to be a prospect. When he asked how old the pitcher was and heard that he was only seventeen, he could not believe it. For years, the Dodgers had been looking for the next Sandy Koufax, the greatest pitcher in Dodgers history and one of the greatest of all time. Brito felt he was looking at the next Koufax.

The Dodgers purchased Valenzuela's contract from Puebla in 1979 and sent Fernando to the minor leagues. He did well but did not throw quite as hard as most major leaguers. The Dodgers believed that as he moved closer to the major leagues, he would need to learn another pitch to succeed.

Valenzuela reminded some people of former Dodgers pitcher and minor league coach Bobby Castillo. Castillo had not thrown very hard either, but he had made up for that by throwing a screwball. When a left-handed pitcher like Castillo throws a curveball, it breaks away from a left-handed hitter, or in to a right-hander. A screwball curves the opposite way—in to a left-handed hitter and away from a righty.

That winter the Dodgers sent Valenzuela and Castillo to the Arizona Instructional League. They asked Castillo to teach Fernando how to throw a screwball.

Soon after the two men arrived in Arizona, they went to the bullpen at the ballpark. After they warmed up with a catcher, Castillo demonstrated the pitch for Fernando. He threw the ball toward the plate, and as he released the ball, he allowed it to roll off the side of his middle finger. That made the ball spin in the opposite direction of a curveball and break the other way.

Castillo showed Fernando how to hold the ball and watched Fernando mimic his grip. Then he had Fernando slowly go through his pitching motion so he could become accustomed to the way he would release the ball. Finally, Castillo motioned for the bullpen catcher to get into a crouch. Castillo was prepared to spend hours with Fernando helping him learn. The coach knew that it usually takes a pitcher months or even years to learn a new pitch.

Fernando took his now familiar wind-up and threw the ball to the catcher. The pitch darted in the opposite direction of his curveball, just as Castillo's had.

The coach was dumbfounded. Never had he seen a pitcher learn so fast. "Valenzuela picked it up right away," he said later. "He has a very loose arm, just right for a screwball." Within a week Fernando was throwing the pitch as if he had been doing so for years, and he was able to use it in games.

Fernando was hard to hit already, but the new pitch, combined with his unique wind-up, made him even tougher. Despite his lack of experience he raced through the Dodgers farm system and late in the 1980 season was called up to the big leagues for the first time. As the Dodgers fought the Astros for the division title before losing in a playoff, Fernando was perfect. In several relief appearances he did not give up an earned run.

Still, when Fernando went to spring training and made the team in 1981 at age twenty, many people in baseball thought he had just been lucky. Surely, they said, major league hitters would soon figure him out and learn how to hit him.

But five days after pitching his opening day shutout, in his next start in San Francisco, Fernando was almost as good, giving up only one run and earning a 7–1 win. Five days later in San Diego he threw a shutout against the Padres, and in Houston he faced the Astros for the second time in three weeks. They were no more success-ful than they had been the first time—Fernando shut them out again.

By the time he took the mound in Dodger Stadium for the second time of the season on April 27, the stands were full. But the crowd was a little different than usual.

Normally, the crowd at Dodger Stadium is a little laid-back. Because of the heavy Los Angeles traffic, fans tend to arrive late and leave early. It takes a lot to get them excited.

But on this day the crowd started showing up hours before the game. Fans waited in long lines for tickets. And for the first time anyone could remember, there were thou-sands and thousands of Mexican American and Latino fans in the stands. Some carried the Mexican flag and waved it proudly, and groups of Latino fans were singing and chant-ing as they did at soccer games.

For the first time since the Dodgers had moved to Los Angeles, Mexican American fans in southern California had someone to cheer for. They finally had a player who made the Dodgers feel like their team, and made them feel welcome in Chavez Ravine again.

Valenzuela did not disappoint his fans, shutting out the Giants 5–0, his fifth victory of the season against no defeats, with four of those five wins by shutout. When he finally gave up an earned run, it was his first in fifty-four innings!

Fernando was even getting big hits himself at the plate. Watching him play seemed like witnessing history. No one could remember another player ever getting off to such a quick start. One newspaper columnist wrote that it was like seeing the great slugger Babe Ruth "when he was just a few months out of the orphanage . . . or Willie Mays in his first season at the Polo Grounds."

Other writers were not so kind. They stereotyped Fernando, making up stories based on the kind of person they imagined a Mexican to be. One wrote that after each game he "went out in search of a burrito." Another nicknamed him Chief because some of his ancestors were Mexican Indians. Others assumed that because he was Mexican, he was stupid and was successful only because he did not really understand that he was pitching in the big leagues. They said Fernando was a poor athlete who was just lucky. In reality, he was a terrific athlete—he could even dribble baseballs with his feet and legs, a skill he had learned from playing soccer. And he knew exactly what was happening. After a game he usually went back to his hotel room. Fernando was smart enough to know that he needed his rest and that if he went out on the streets, he would be mobbed by fans. What the papers were beginning to refer to as Fernandomania was just getting started.

That became obvious one day in early May. Before the start of the season the Dodgers scheduled Fernando and several other players to appear at a clinic in a park in East Los Angeles. Usually, only a few hundred kids showed up at such clinics, where Dodger players signed autographs and gave a few tips on how to play ball.

But when Fernando arrived, thousands of fans were waiting for him. News helicopters were flying overhead, and dozens of photographers were eager to take his picture. The other players were ignored. Fernando had to be led around the park by police to keep his fans from smothering him. He passed out hundreds of autographed pictures and took dozens of questions, with Mike Brito acting as his translator.

One question gave some insight into just how aware Fernando was about everything that was going on. "Fernando," someone asked, "are you rich or poor?"

The young pitcher paused for a moment. Growing up in Mexico, Fernando had been very poor. Now he was beginning to make a lot of money, and he knew that if he kept pitching well, he would soon be rich. He hoped to fulfill his dream of building his parents a new home. In fact, he already had hired an agent to help him take financial advantage of his popularity. But he answered the question thoughtfully, showing that he was wise enough to know that money is not the answer to everything. He said, "It doesn't matter what position in life you have, if you have the qualities needed to play ball." Rich or poor, he explained, if you loved what you did, the way he loved baseball, you could still be happy.

Meanwhile, the crowd had grown so big that Fernando finally had to hide in a ladies' room for a chance to breathe. That was Fernandomania. He was the biggest story in baseball, and that season he helped the Dodgers zoom into first place.

Fernando won eight games in a row before he lost his first game of the season. He then struggled in his next two starts before returning to form.

In the meantime, however, baseball fans found themselves distracted by something else. In the off-season the union representing the players had begun to argue with baseball's owners over their contract. Now negotiations between the two sides broke down, and on June 12, with the Dodgers in first place in their division with a record of

36–21—nine of those wins by Fernando—the players went on strike.

The season screeched to a halt. Week after week ballparks all around the country sat empty and fans grew frustrated. Some said that even when baseball resumed, they did not plan to go back to the ballpark.

The strike was finally settled at the end of July. The season was scheduled to start again on August 10, after a few days of practice.

Although many fans were happy that the strike was over, others picketed ballparks and planned to boycott the games. Fans who did attend games sometimes carried protest signs or banners accusing both the owners and players of thinking only of themselves. "What about the fans?" they asked. Everyone in the game wondered whether fans would come out to see baseball for the rest of the season, and just as many wondered whether Fernando could continue his amazing performance.

Both questions were soon answered. In the Dodgers' first game after the strike, there were more than fifteen thousand empty seats in Dodger Stadium, one of the smallest crowds of the season. But the next night, with Fernando scheduled to pitch, the game was almost a sellout.

When he took the mound, everyone forgot the strike. As a rookie, Fernando was only making $45,000 a year, and the fans didn't blame him for the trouble between the owners and the players.

Although Fernando was a little rusty, he left the game with the lead. In his next start the Dodgers had their first sellout since the strike. While some teams had trouble drawing big crowds, wherever Fernando pitched, fans of every background forgot about being mad and turned out to watch. For the remainder of the season, Dodger Stadium was sold out every game he pitched. If not for Fernando, baseball might not have recovered from the strike and won back so many fans.

Although Fernando did not pitch quite as well in the second half of the season, he finished with thirteen wins and led the Dodgers to the postseason. And he had just as big an impact off the field. In Latin America the number of radio stations that carried Dodgers games doubled from twenty to forty. In Mexico alone the number of stations that broadcast Dodgers games went from three to seventeen. Almost overnight the Dodgers became the most popular team in Latin America. In his native Mexico everyone was proud of Fernando, and in southern California the Mexican American community burst with pride over his accomplishments. For the first time many young Mexican Americans and Latinos had someone to look up to.

The Dodgers made the playoffs. Because of the strike there was an added round of playoffs that year. The Dodgers, who had been in first place in the division before the strike, had to play their archrivals, the Astros, who had been in first place after the strike.

Fernando was manager Lasorda's selection to pitch the first game against the Astros and their great pitcher Nolan Ryan. The player who had been an emergency fill-in on opening day was now the ace of the staff.

For some fans watching on national television, it would be their first chance to see Fernando. They were not disappointed. He was great, and baffled the Astros yet again, giving up no runs. But Nolan Ryan was a little bit better. He gave up only two hits. The Astros scored off the Dodgers' relief pitchers and won, 3–1.

Houston won the next game and took a commanding two-game lead in the playoffs. But the Dodgers fought back to win the next game. Even though Fernando would not have as much rest as usual, manager Lasorda asked him if he could pitch the next game.

Fernando said he could. This time, Fernando was determined to win.

The capacity crowd at Dodger Stadium roared when they saw Fernando stride out to the bullpen before the game, and Mexican flags waved throughout the ballpark. In the stands, fans of every background, Latino and American and everything in between, sat side by side and cheered every pitch, united by their love of Fernando and the Dodgers.

Despite the unusually short rest, Fernando pitched as if he had rested all winter. As *Los Angeles Times* sportswriter Mark Heisler commented, "Fernando's last stand went down as had all his other stands: a sellout, a masterpiece, some modesty on his part, some awe on everyone else's part, a couple of *bueno*s . . . and then he was gone, leaving the world to wonder." Fernando had a perfect game through five innings and a shutout until the ninth inning. He gave up only four hits, and the Dodgers beat the Astros 2–1.

"There was no way," said manager Lasorda, "I was going to take him out of the game in the ninth inning. . . . Sometimes when I look at him I think I'm dreaming."

Bur Fernando was no dream. "I think I have pitched a couple better games," Fernando said afterward, "but this was the most important game for the team."

Then one reporter asked, "Why are you never nervous?"

"I don't know," answered Fernando. "I can't explain it. It is just the natural way to be."

The Dodgers won the next game to advance in the play-offs. Fernando pitched and won the final game, and the Dodgers defeated the Montreal Expos in five games to win the pennant and the right to play the powerful New York Yankees in the World Series.

The Yankees were heavy favorites and won the first two games of the World Series in New York. After the two teams traveled to Los Angeles for the third game, manager Lasorda once more put a brand-new baseball in Fernando's glove in his locker. It was a must-win game.

Dodger Stadium was in the full swing of Fernandomania when Fernando took the mound for game three. But for the first time all year, it seemed as if he was finally running out of steam. In the first inning he struggled, walking two batters before finally escaping. In the bottom of the first the Dodgers gave him a break and scored three runs. That was usually plenty for Valenzuela. But not today.

In the second inning the Yankees scored twice, one run on a leadoff home run by Bob Watson and another after two hits. Lasorda started a pitcher warming up in the bullpen, but Valenzuela worked his way out of a jam, stranding two runners.

In the third inning Fernando gave up another home run. The Dodgers now trailed 4–3. Fernando had been pitching a Cinderella season, but it looked as if the clock was about to strike twelve.

Yet Fernando refused to give up. He pitched from behind in the count. He shook off his catcher over and over again. He worked slowly and stepped off the mound time after time as if to rest, drawing energy from a crowd that would not stop cheering and would not let him lose. He faltered again and again and again. But he did not fall.

Manager Lasorda stuck with his ace pitcher. In the middle of the game he decided that no matter what happened, he was not going to take Fernando out. "I thought about it," he said later, "but this is the year of Fernando."

The Dodgers scored two runs in the fifth inning to take a 5–4 lead, and for the next three innings Fernando was a magician as the Yankees repeatedly threatened to score only to have him stop them again and again.

By the ninth inning Fernandomania was at a fever pitch. The Dodgers crowd was on its feet the whole inning after Fernando took the mound. He had already thrown 131 pitches. And like a matador at a bullfight in his native country, he kept dodging danger.

On his 145th pitch of the night, he spun and looked to the sky once more and poured another pitch over the strike zone. Lou Piniella, the last Yankees hitter, struck out. The crowd roared, and Fernando's teammates swarmed over him on the mound. "That," said Lasorda, "was one of the gutsiest performances I've ever seen a young man do. He was like a poker player bluffing his way through a hand."

Although Fernando did not pitch again in the series, the Dodgers were inspired by the victory and went on to win the next three games and the world championship. When the 1981 season was over, Fernando won both the Cy Young Award as the National League's best pitcher and the Rookie of the Year Award. He went on to pitch seventeen seasons in the major leagues, with 173 wins. Then he returned to Mexico and pitched several more seasons in his home country before retiring from baseball.

Even though Fernando has retired, his impact on the game can still be seen today in every ballpark in the major leagues. Jaime Jarrin, the Dodgers' Spanish language broadcaster, estimated that before Fernando joined the Dodgers, fewer than ten percent of the crowd in Dodger Stadium was Latino. But after Fernando joined the Dodgers, nearly one-third of the people in the stands were Latino Americans. They became Dodger fans and fans of big league baseball, and even after Fernando left the Dodgers and eventually retired from baseball, they remained fans of the game.

By becoming such a big star and revealing how many

Latinos were fans of baseball, Valenzuela helped all Latino players and made baseball even more popular. Today Latino players are on the roster of every big league team. They are some of the biggest stars in the game, such as slugger Albert Pujols of the St. Louis Cardinals and closer Mariano Rivera of the New York Yankees. Latino players are treated much better by both their teams and the press, and Latino fans are in the stands of every major league ballpark.

America has been called a nation of immigrants. Fernando Valenzuela, a pudgy young man from Mexico, helped make baseball a game for everyone, and truly our national pastime.

ILA BORDERS

FOR LOVE OF THE GAME

ALL ILA BORDERS EVER WANTED TO DO was play baseball.

When her father, Phil Borders, was a young man, he dreamed of pitching in the major leagues. His wife Marianne shared his love of the game. Their daughter Ila was born in 1975. There was nothing Ila enjoyed more than cuddling with her parents on the couch watching baseball on television, or going into the backyard with them and playing with a wiffle ball and bat.

When Ila was about five years old, she began playing softball in the local girls' league. From the very beginning, Phil sensed that his daughter was special. Unlike most children—including most boys—Ila was never afraid of the ball, and when her father showed her how to grip the bat or field a ground ball, she imitated him almost exactly.

A left-handed thrower like her dad, Ila could already throw the ball accurately all the way across the diamond by the time she was seven. She was big for her age, and a good player, but Ila knew that softball wasn't the same as baseball. Still, she never really wondered why she wasn't playing baseball. That was a game that seemed to be for boys only.

Then, one day when Ila was ten years old, her dad took her to see the Dodgers play.

Watching a major league game in person is much better than watching it on television. As Ila watched the Dodgers play, she found herself imagining that she was on the mound in front of a big crowd that cheered every pitch. On the way home, as she daydreamed about playing in the major leagues, she told her dad that she didn't want to play softball anymore. She wanted to play baseball, and she really wanted to be a pitcher, just like her dad.

Most fathers probably would have explained to their daughter that baseball is a boys' game and that women are not strong enough to play. But Phil Borders could think of no reason why Ila could not, or should not, play baseball and try to pitch. She already had a good arm, and she was left-handed, which Phil knew is a real advantage for a pitcher, because hitters see so few pitchers throwing with their left hand. He thought that "left-handed pitchers don't grow on trees," and that Ila might actually have a chance to be pretty good. Like him, she had big hands that would make it easy to hold a baseball.

"Okay," her father told her, "if you want to play baseball, you can, and if you want to pitch, I'll teach you how."

The rest of the way home, Ila's daydreams got even bigger.

Women have always played baseball, just not very often and usually not against men. During the early days of the game there were occasionally teams of all-women players, but over time most women ballplayers, like Ila, were steered toward other sports. Baseball was considered too rough and tough for girls.

Still, there were always women who refused to give up their love of the game. From about 1905 through 1920, Alta Weiss pitched semiprofessional baseball in northeastern Ohio. Another woman, Jackie Mitchell, signed a contract to play for the minor league Chattanooga Lookouts in 1931 and pitched in an exhibition game against Babe Ruth and Lou Gehrig of the New York Yankees, striking out both players. But a few days later the commissioner of baseball, Kenesaw Mountain Landis, ended Jackie's career. He declared that baseball was "too strenuous" for women and canceled her contract. Organized baseball, which includes the major leagues and the minor leagues affiliated with them, eventually instituted a rule that banned women from playing.

But it was impossible to stop women from playing baseball on teams and in leagues outside the control of the baseball commissioner. Mamie Johnson and Toni Stone both played in the Negro Leagues in the 1950s, and from 1943 through 1954 the All-American Girls Professional Baseball League played throughout the Midwest. In 1950 Kathryn Johnston played Little League baseball, but in 1951 Little League ruled that "girls are not eligible under any conditions." That didn't change until after Maria Pepe tried to play Little League in Hoboken, New Jersey, in 1972. She was forced to quit after playing only three games, but two years later a court ruling gave girls everywhere the right to play Little League. Since that time legal bans against female players have been lifted virtually everywhere. Today, nothing can prevent a female from playing in professional organized baseball except her own ability.

Still, although thousands of girls play Little League

today, very few continue to play baseball when they get older. Fortunately, Ila did not know that. All she knew was that she loved baseball and she loved to play.

Ila's dad knew that if she wanted to pitch, she would have to practice, and as a former pitcher himself, he knew how to teach her. Every Friday afternoon Ila would call her dad at his automobile paint shop and ask him when he was coming home to play. Every Friday evening and every weekend morning was practice time for Ila.

Phil would take his daughter to a local park. First he would pitch to her, getting her accustomed to hitting balls tossed overhand rather than underhand, as in softball. Then he would show Ila how to pitch.

He showed her how to wrap her fingers around the ball correctly, holding it across the stitches with her first two fingers and placing her thumb beneath it. And he showed her how to stand on the mound with one foot on the pitching rubber, and how to wind up and throw toward the plate, following through and then ending in position to field the ball.

Ila's dad sometimes shot video of her pitching and then showed her what she was doing wrong. When they watched games together, he explained to her what the pitcher must be thinking on the mound. He didn't try to teach her how to throw curveballs or any trick pitches. That could come later. He knew that the most important skill for a pitcher to learn is control.

Ila loved it, but three days of practice was not nearly enough for her. The Borders lived in California, and the weather was nice enough to play every day. Ila drew a strike zone on the brick wall of her house and spent hour after hour throwing the ball against the wall and pretending she was in the World Series, pitching in front of thousands of people. As she later recalled, "I marked the wall, outside, knee high, and up and in, and played a little game. I tried to hit those spots. It taught me good control."

When Phil believed that his daughter was ready for Little League, he tried to sign her up. Even though girls were allowed on the teams, no girl had ever tried to play Little League in their neighborhood, and league officials were not eager to let Ila join. In fact, they tried to prevent her from doing so by changing the location of the sign-ups without telling her father. But he and Ila were determined. They finally tracked down the sign-ups, and Ila registered to play.

Like all potential Little League players, Ila had to try out. As soon as the coaches saw her play, they knew that she could hit and throw as well as any boy, and better than most.

Ila's teammates, who all knew her from school and already knew she was a good player from the playground, did not think twice about playing baseball with a girl. Unfortunately, some parents were not so open-minded and would heckle her during games, particularly when she was on the mound striking out hitter after hitter. Little League mothers, Ila later recalled, "were the toughest on me." One told her to "go back to Barbie dolls." Another said she should "stick with your tea party."

The words stung, but Ila tried not to let anything that happened on the baseball field make her feel bad. "My dad said something that stuck with me," she once told a reporter. "He said, 'If you let things bother you, you're not made for this game.'"

The more she played, the clearer it became that Ila was made for the game. She was named to the All-Star team and in one game struck out eighteen hitters in six innings. When she entered Whittier Christian Junior High School she tried out for the baseball team and made it easily. Her team went undefeated during her seventh and eighth grades, and Ila was named the team MVP. Over the course of two seasons she pitched forty innings, struck out seventy hitters, and only gave up a couple of runs.

She loved every minute of it. When she told her coach, Ron Esslinger, that she wanted to pitch in the major leagues, he did not laugh. Instead, he encouraged her. He told her that if she kept working hard and kept improving, anything was possible.

When Ila turned fourteen and graduated from junior high, her father felt that it was time for her to understand just how difficult it would be to continue pitching as an adult. In Little League the pitcher's mound is only forty-five feet from home plate. But high school fields are the same size as those in professional baseball. Ila would have to learn to pitch from a distance of sixty feet six inches from home plate, just like they did in the major leagues.

To prepare her, that summer Ila's father helped her join a semipro team so she could play against and with grown men. Since she couldn't throw quite as hard as some male pitchers, she had to learn to pitch smarter. Instead of throwing fastballs past hitters, Ila had to use her brain, throwing to different spots, changing speeds, using her control, and fooling the hitters. She quickly adapted and held her own against these older players.

She wanted to pitch for her local high school, but under the rules of Title IX, the government regulations on the rights of women to compete in sports in school, since the school had a girls' softball team, it did not have to allow her to play on the boys' baseball team, and so it banned her from trying out.

Ila and her father were disappointed, but nothing could stop her. She enrolled at a private school, Whittier Christian High School, and earned a place on the freshman team before being promoted to the varsity team later in the year. Local newspapers were intrigued and sometimes sent reporters to cover the games when she pitched. While she wasn't as dominant as she had been in junior high school, she was still one of the better players on the field.

And there was no one more dedicated. Ila knew that as a woman, she was not as big and strong as many of her teammates and opponents. So every morning she rose at five a.m. to run and lift weights.

Once again Ila was accepted by her teammates, many of whom had played with her or against her in junior high school or summer leagues. And when players for the opposition tried to show her up by blowing her kisses from the batter's box or acting disrespectful in other ways, Ila knew what to do. "I just brush them back," she later told a reporter, meaning she threw the ball close to them. "It's my favorite pitch."

Surprisingly, the people who gave her the most trouble were girls her own age.

Some of her female friends didn't understand why she did not want to play softball with them. Others were resentful that, because she was on the baseball team, she spent more time with their boyfriends than they did. Still others were simply jealous of all the attention Ila received. Sometimes when Ila struck out a batter on the opposing team, she was threatened by the hitter's girlfriend. Once in a while she even had to be escorted to her car after a game so she wouldn't be attacked.

Ila tried to keep everything in perspective and follow her father's advice to not allow anything to bother her. "I know it's kind of weird, a girl playing baseball," she said, "but I love it so much I can't see going without it."

Each time she took the mound, her teammates found themselves agreeing with her. Her four-year high school record was a stellar 16–7, including a no-hitter, with 165 strikeouts in 147 innings, and as a senior she was named team MVP and was a first team all-league selection.

Also during her senior year Ila was contacted by several college coaches interested in knowing whether she was interested in continuing her baseball career in college. Although a handful of women had played college baseball and even pitched a few innings, no woman had ever been recruited to play college baseball on a scholarship.

Ila was intrigued, but she and her parents were also cautious. They were afraid that some schools were interested in Ila only for the publicity she attracted. They also wanted to make sure that the school recognized that Ila would need some special treatment. She couldn't use the same locker room as her male teammates. They wanted to make sure her coach valued her as a pitcher first and was committed to helping Ila realize her dream of pitching professionally. After doing some research, they sent tapes of Ila pitching in high school to ten small colleges.

Fortunately, they found one school and one coach that seemed perfect for Ila. Charlie Phillips, a former professional pitcher himself and the coach for Southern California College, a small Christian school, had followed Ila's career closely. As impressed as he was with her as a pitcher, he was even more impressed with her as a person. When she was still in high school, he had told his wife, "I'm going to sign that kid someday. She's something special."

When Ila graduated from high school, Phillips made

good on his promise and offered her a partial scholarship to play baseball. Southern California College played in the Golden State League with small colleges in California. Although the competition was not as good as that at many bigger colleges, a few SCC players had played professionally, and one, Tim Fortugno, was a pitcher in the major leagues. Most players in the league had been big high school stars, and Ila knew she would have to play her best in order to compete.

Thus far, although a few local newspapers had written stories about Ila, she had not attracted very much media attention. That would soon change.

When Ila began practicing with the SCC team, she immediately impressed coach Phillips. She was serious about the game, and it showed. She stood five foot ten and weighed about 160 pounds, a bit small for a pitcher, but she wasn't the smallest player on the team. Her fastball came to the plate at about eighty miles per hour, and she could either throw it straight or make it dart in toward a right-handed hitter. She also knew how to throw a changeup, a curveball, and a screwball. While eighty miles per hour is not very fast for a college pitcher, Ila's control was much better than that of other pitchers on the team. Although there were a few awkward moments at first, as the players got to know her, she became just another member of the team.

She was scheduled to make her first start for SCC on February 15, 1994, against Claremont-Mudd College. Usually SCC games attracted only a dozen or so spectators, most of them parents of the players.

Ila was so excited that she barely slept the night before the game. And when she got to the ballpark she could hardly believe her eyes. The national media had heard that a girl was going to pitch a college baseball game, and all of a sudden Ila was big news. Hundreds of fans packed the bleachers and lined the outfield. Newspaper photographers jostled one another for a good spot behind the backstop, and several television cameramen followed Ila's every move. Reporters from newspapers all around the country walked around interviewing fans and players.

As Ila warmed up, she tried to stay calm. Seeing a woman pitch might have been big news to everyone else, but it was completely normal to Ila. She couldn't wait to take the mound.

When she did, she threw a few warm-up tosses to her catcher, Dave Seeley; then, as the crowd started cheering for her, she tried to block it all out and just concentrate on throwing strikes. The Claremont hitter, Gabe Rosenthal, dug in. Ila's catcher flashed the signs between his legs and Ila gave a small nod. She knew Rosenthal did not want to make an out to a girl.

In her blue and white pinstriped uniform and cap, she looked just like any other player—except for the long ponytail trailing down her back.

The catcher signaled for a curveball. Ila set her fingers on the ball, wound up, and whipped her arm toward the plate.

The ball spun in the air and then started to curve to the ground. Her catcher caught it at his shoe tops. Ball one.

The pitch had been low, but some people in the crowd were already impressed. They had not believed that a woman could throw a curveball.

Ila took another sign. Fastball. The catcher tapped his leg to let Ila know he wanted the pitch on the corner.

She stared at the target and wound up again. This time she let the ball spin off the tips of her fingers.

Perfect! The ball caught the edge of the plate as the hitter watched it pass. The umpire's right arm shot up in the air. "Stee-rike one!" he called out.

Then Ila threw a third pitch. This time the batter swung.

Dink! The aluminum bat hit the ball and sent it toward center field.

Ila wasn't worried. She had played enough baseball to know the sound of a routine fly ball. She watched the lazy fly soar over her head and then drop into the glove of her centerfielder.

Out. Ila Borders had just made history by becoming the first woman to pitch in an official college game. But she didn't just want to pitch—she wanted to win!

Mixing her pitches beautifully and maintaining excellent control, Ila kept Claremont off balance. She didn't get into trouble until the fourth inning. With two outs, there were two runners on base.

In the stands, some fans started nudging each other and whispering. A few thought she'd just been lucky in the first few innings and expected her to blow up and give up a bunch of runs.

Ila knew better. Pitching carefully, she got two strikes on the hitter and then hit the corner for the first strikeout of the day.

As the game went on, she only got stronger. Meanwhile, her teammates banged out hit after hit. At the end of the game the scoreboard read SCC 12, CLAREMONT 1. Claremont scored their only run in the eighth inning on a home run by Rosenthal, the first hitter Ila had faced.

Ila was thrilled. As she ran off the field, her teammates

surrounded her and poured a bucket of Gatorade over her head in celebration. Reporters swarmed around her and, over the next day, Ila gave more than seventy interviews. "All I can say right now" said Ila to one, "is that I am happy beyond belief."

Everyone was impressed. Gabe Rosenthal told a reporter, "She's a good pitcher. She threw a lot of junk, but she's always around the dish. I think she'll do well. She'll win again. . . . After she was getting everybody out I think people realized she was a pretty good baseball player and forgot she was a girl." That was exactly what Ila wanted to hear. Although she understood that as a woman playing baseball against men she was a trailblazer, that was not the reason she was playing. "I'm not here for the publicity," she told a reporter. "I'm just out here for the love of the game."

Over the remainder of the season, Ila continued to prove that she was no sideshow attraction. A short time later she pitched and won a three-hitter against Concordia, and although she lost her next four games, she finished the season with an earned run average (the average number of runs given up in nine innings) of 2.92. "My goal going into the season was to keep my ERA under three," she said, "and I did, so I am pleased."

But at the same time, the season had not been very pleasant. In some games the players on the opposing teams made unkind remarks about her, as did some of the fans. She tried to ignore them and looked toward the example of Jackie Robinson as an inspiration, telling one reporter that "Jackie Robinson dealt with it extremely well. He just went out and did his job. He gives me great hope."

She still dreamed of making it to the big leagues. "You never know how far you are going to go," she said. "You just work your tail off and see what happens."

She looked forward to her sophomore year, but the team lost several important players and struggled, as did Ila. She never got into a good groove and finished the season 1–7 with an ERA of 7.20. Coach Phillips was replaced, and in Ila's junior year the new coach decided to use younger players. Ila was pulled from the starting rotation and pitched only twenty-four innings.

Her dream of playing in the major leagues was slipping away. In the annual draft of amateur players, no major league team selected her or asked her to attend a tryout. She needed to play someplace where she could pitch more. She transferred to Whittier College for her senior year and earned a spot in the starting rotation, pitching in twelve games and compiling a record of 4–5 with a 5.22 ERA.

In her last start of the season she was supposed to pitch against her old team, Southern California College.

Just before the game, however, Ila abruptly withdrew from school. Her college career was over, but her baseball career was about to move to a new stage.

Although major league scouts did not think that Ila threw hard enough to pitch in the major leagues, there are professional leagues known as independent leagues that are not affiliated with organized baseball. Most players in independent ball are either overlooked by organized baseball or are players—including some with major league experience—who are trying to resume their careers after having been released or hurt. Most independent league players hope to attract the attention of big league scouts. More than a few have made it to the major leagues.

In the spring of Ila's senior year in college, she and her father started hearing from independent league teams who were interested in signing Ila to a contract.

Ila was excited, but she was also cautious. She did not want to sign with a team that was just interested in using her to attract publicity, or to draw a big crowd to see her pitch. She wanted to play for a team that was interested in her as a pitcher, not just as a woman.

The St. Paul Saints of the Northern League were the most successful team in the independent leagues and drew bigger crowds than most minor league teams. Their owner, Mike Veeck, was the son of former major league owner Bill Veeck, one of the most innovative and courageous team owners in the history of baseball. When Bill Veeck signed Larry Doby to play for the Cleveland Indians in 1947, Doby broke the color line in the American League and became only the second African American to play in the majors. Mike Veeck was very much like his father, so when he called and asked Ila if she wanted to try out, she was intrigued. The Saints already sold out most of their games, so they didn't need Ila to fill the stands. Although the Saints would not mind the publicity, they were always looking for another pitcher.

Ila knew she could return to school and complete her degree whenever she wanted, but she might never receive another chance to play professional baseball. Shortly after she left college, the Saints invited her to spring training. Ila would have to pitch her way onto the team, of course; she was just one of dozens of players trying out. Every time she pitched, she had to do her best, but if she made the team, she would earn about $1,000 a month.

Her first test came in an exhibition game against the

Duluth-Superior Dukes. Ila came into the game in relief in the seventh inning. The crowd of nearly four thousand fans gave her a long standing ovation.

Ila took the mound and quickly threw her warm-up pitches. A left-handed batter, Jeff Jensen, stepped into the box. Jensen was an important hitter for Ila. Manager Marty Scott of the Saints told her that he would probably use her to get out left-handers—if she proved she could do it. And Jensen wasn't just any old left-handed hitter. He was in his third year in the league and had hit .295 the previous season.

The experienced hitter was patient. Ila threw one pitch for a strike, then two balls, and then another strike. Jensen had yet to move the bat from his shoulder.

Ila and her catcher decided to trick him. They guessed that Jensen would not want to strike out against Ila on a called third strike and would be eager to swing. They decided to throw a changeup, a pitch that looks like a fastball but is slower.

Ila threw a perfect pitch. Jensen started to swing, then, before he could stop, realized he was way ahead of the pitch. His bat flailed across the plate a split second before the ball.

Strike three!

The fans, wrote one reporter, "went bonkers," chanting, "Ila! Ila! Ila!," over and over. The next hitter grounded out, and then Ila gave up a walk, but the last batter hit another weak ground ball to an infielder. Although it was only an exhibition game, Ila had pitched a complete inning in pro baseball without giving up a run!

The next inning didn't go quite as well, however. With two outs and the bases loaded, a Saints outfielder missed a fly ball and several runs scored. But Ila also recorded two more strikeouts that inning. "She did a whale of a job," said her catcher. A few days later manager Scott told her she had made the team. Although she kept her emotions under control in front of her coach, when she went back to her room, she couldn't help herself. "I went nuts," she said later. "I was jumping on the bed and calling everybody."

Ila could not wait for the season to begin. Her whole life, she had dreamed of pitching in a professional game.

Two games into the season, she got her chance. In the sixth inning, with two runners on and a left-handed batter at the plate, manager Scott went to the mound and waved Ila into the game.

Ila trotted in from the bullpen and took the mound as the crowd cheered. Eight minutes later she trotted off. This time she heard some boos.

///

She had been terrible. Her first pitch had hit the batter, and then she committed a balk, which allowed one run to score. Next she fielded a ground ball and threw it away for an error, and then she gave up another hit. After only twelve pitches Scott pulled her from the game.

Ila was disappointed but tried to keep things in perspective. "That's life, I guess," she said. "Whatever doesn't kill you makes you stronger."

Over the next few weeks Ila continued to struggle. Some observers said she didn't belong in pro baseball. With the Saints fighting for the pennant, management had to make a change.

She was traded to the Duluth-Superior Dukes. The Dukes needed pitchers, and Mike Veeck thought Ila might do better if she was under a little less pressure.

Ila was determined to do better. She now realized she was playing for more than herself. At every game her team played, the stands were full of girls and boys who wanted to see Ila pitch and who had their own dreams. After each game hundreds of these young fans would be waiting for her autograph, and each day she got dozens of letters, mostly from young girls and women, telling her to keep playing.

And then there were the people who still believed that neither Ila nor any other woman had the right to play baseball. She received threatening letters, and some fans still called her terrible names. One manager in the Northern League would not even say her name—he just called her "that thing." She needed to prove these people wrong.

After ten days with the Dukes, Ila finally got her chance. With the team trailing 6–3, Ila came on in relief in the ninth inning.

Once again, everyone in the stands rose to their feet and applauded as she warmed up. This time, Ila wanted them to be cheering her just as hard when she left the game.

The first batter Ila would face had already collected two hits in the game, and now he worked the count to two balls and two strikes. Ila's catcher signaled for a curveball. She wound up and threw the pitch, but instead of curving, the ball just spun in the air. She had thrown the pitch poorly; it was a "hanging" curveball, one that doesn't curve.

The batter lashed the ball past Ila and into center field for a single.

Ila took a deep breath. She knew she was lucky that he had not hit a home run.

With a runner on first, Ila worked the next hitter carefully. If she kept the ball low, he might hit a ground ball for a double play.

Ila knew her curveball wasn't working very well, so she used her fastball to get ahead of the hitter. Then she threw a changeup, hoping to fool him. Sure enough, the pitch surprised him. At the last second he lunged at the pitch and bounced a slow ground ball to the second baseman. The second baseman flipped the ball to the shortstop, who touched second just before the runner slid in, then threw hard to first base. The throw just beat the runner.

Double play! Ila pumped her fist—she felt like doing a cartwheel, but she didn't dare. She still had a hitter to get out.

The next batter was Nate Vopata, a veteran player who had played in the minor leagues the previous year. He was hoping to get back into organized baseball, and earlier in the year had a hit a long home run off Ila when she was pitching for St. Paul. And today he was having a terrific game. He had already hit a single, a double, and a triple. He needed only a home run to complete what is known as the cycle, one of each kind of hit in the same game. Hitting for the cycle is a rare accomplishment that can get the attention of major league scouts. Ila knew Vopata would try his best to hit a home run and not take it easy on her.

But Ila did not want him or anyone else to go easy on her. She wanted to succeed or fail on her own.

The last time she had faced Vopata, he had hit a home run off a fastball. She figured that would be the last pitch he would be looking for now, so when her catcher called a fastball, she nodded.

Ila wound up and threw, aiming for the outside edge of the plate.

Too late, Vopata recognized the pitch as a fastball and swung. His bat barely hit the ball for a foul strike!

Now Ila figured that Vopata would probably be looking for a changeup. After all, that was the pitch she had used to get the previous hitter out. To catch him off guard, she decided to go with the curveball. Although she had hung the last one, she knew she could do better. She had to.

The crowd was on their feet, cheering for Ila as if she were pitching in the World Series. It was just as Ila had imagined when she attended her first big league game or threw pitch after pitch at the brick wall. She tried to stay calm and concentrate.

She wound up and threw. The ball spun through the air, straight at Vopata's shoulder. Then it suddenly curved down over the plate.

Vopata swung, but he was a little late and hit the ball

off the skinny part of the bat next to his hands. It rolled weakly to the second baseman, who fielded the ball and threw to first for the out.

Ila had done it! She had thrown a shutout inning in professional baseball. No one, ever, would be able to say she didn't belong.

Ila finished the season with the Dukes and played for the team again in 1998 and 1999. In 1998 she won her first game and on two occasions pitched six full innings of shutout baseball. Shortly after the start of the 1999 season, she was traded to the Madison Black Wolf and pitched the best baseball of her career, finishing the season with an ERA of 3.63, well under the league average, and becoming, without question, the most successful female pitcher in the history of baseball.

But even to Ila it soon became clear that even though she was talented, she simply did not throw hard enough to play in the big leagues. In 2000 she pitched a few games for the Zion Pioneerzz, in the Western League, but then she made the decision to retire. Playing in the minor leagues and traveling all the time was a hard life. She had given the game everything she had, but at age twenty-six, and still needing a few more courses for her college degree, Ila decided it was time to get on with her life and finish school.

"I'll look back and say I did something nobody else ever did," she told a reporter. "I'm proud of that. I wasn't out to prove women's rights or anything. I love baseball.

"Although I've been spit on and sworn at," she said, "the memories I have are the ovations when I would run in from the bullpen.

"I happen to think it's pretty fantastic that I'm the only female to play baseball with the guys."

And while Ila may have been the first woman to pitch in professional baseball, she will most certainly not be the last. Her example demonstrates that if girls have the desire and the ability, they can play baseball. Because of Ila, the next woman to play professional baseball will know what to expect and will have an easier time. After all, Ila showed everyone just how far a person can go when she plays for the love of the game. Like Hank Greenberg, Jackie Robinson, and Fernando Valenzuela, by breaking a barrier, Ila Borders helped make baseball a game for everyone.

SOURCES AND FURTHER READING

When I am writing a book, I use many, many different sources, including newspaper stories, magazine articles, books, video documentaries, and the Internet.

If you would like to read more about any of the athletes in this book, your teacher or school or town librarian can probably show you how to find newspaper and magazine articles online. You might also want to check out the books listed below, many of which were helpful to me. They can be purchased online or through any bookstore. They might also be in your local library. If not, your library may be able to borrow them for you from another library.

Ask your librarian for help, and happy reading!

HANK GREENBERG

Berkow, Ira. *Hank Greenberg: Hall of Fame Slugger*. Philadelphia: The Jewish Publication Society, 2001.

Berkow, Ira, ed. *Hank Greenberg: The Story of My Life*. Chicago: Triumph Books, 2001.

You might also enjoy reading about Sandy Koufax, Jewish pitching star for the Los Angeles Dodgers.

JACKIE ROBINSON

There are many wonderful books about Jackie Robinson. Here are just a few:

Christopher, Matt, and Glenn Stout. *Jackie Robinson.* Boston: Little, Brown Books for Young Readers, 2004.

Falkner, David. *Great Time Coming: The Life of Jackie Robinson from Baseball to Birmingham.* New York: Touchstone Books, 1995.

Robinson, Jackie. *I Never Had It Made.* New York: Echo Press, 1997.

Stout, Glenn, and Richard A. Johnson. *The Dodgers: 120 Years of Baseball.* Boston: Houghton Mifflin, 2004.

Stout, Glenn, and Dick Johnson. *Jackie Robinson: Between the Baselines.* San Francisco: Woodford Press, 1997.

Tygiel, Jules. *The Jackie Robinson Reader.* New York: Penguin Books, 1998.

FERNANDO VALENZUELA

Unfortunately, although there were several books written about Fernando Valenzuela in the early 1980s, they are no longer in print and are very hard to find. But you can read about Fernando in these books about the Dodgers, and you might also enjoy reading about Latino stars like Roberto Clemente, Albert Pujols, and others.

Stout, Glenn, and Richard A. Johnson. *The Dodgers: 120 Years of Baseball.* Boston: Houghton Mifflin, 2004.

Delsohn, Steve. *True Blue: The Dramatic History of the Los Angeles Dodgers, Told by the Men Who Lived It.* New York: HarperCollins, 2001.

ILA BORDERS

No one has written an entire book about Ila Borders, but for more stories about women and baseball, check out the books listed below. You may also want to watch the movie *A League of Their Own,* directed by Penny Marshall, starring Tom Hanks and Madonna, about the All-American Girls Professional Baseball League.

Ardell, Jean Hastings, with a foreword by Ila Borders. *Breaking into Baseball: Women and the National Pastime.* Carbondale: Southern Illinois University Press, 2005.

Macy, Sue. *A Whole New Ball Game: The Story of the All-American Girls Professional Baseball League.* New York: Puffin Books, 1995.

Ring, Jennifer. *Stolen Bases: Why American Girls Don't Play Baseball.* Chicago: University of Illinois Press, 2009.

For more information about upcoming titles in the "Good Sports" series or about author Glenn Stout, or to contact Glenn about making an author visit to your school or school district, please visit the "Good Sports" Web site: www.goodsportsbyglennstout.com.

And remember, always be a good sport.

Keep reading,

Glenn

ABOUT THE AUTHOR

When Glenn Stout was growing up outside a small town in central Ohio, he never dreamed that he would become a writer. Then reading changed his life. As a kid, Glenn played baseball, basketball, and football, but baseball was always his favorite sport. Glenn studied poetry and creative writing in college and has had many different jobs, including selling minor league baseball tickets, cleaning offices, grading papers for a college, and painting houses. He also worked as a construction worker and a librarian. Glenn started writing professionally while he was working at the Boston Public Library and has been a full-time writer since 1993. Under the auspices of Matt Christopher, Glenn wrote forty titles in the Matt Christopher sports biography series, and every year he edits *The Best American Sports Writing* collection. Some of Glenn's other books include *Red Sox Century, Yankees Century, Nine Months at Ground Zero,* and *Young Woman and the Sea: How Trudy Ederle Conquered the English Channel and Inspired the World.* He has written or edited more than seventy books.

Glenn is a citizen of both the United States and Canada and lives on Lake Champlain in Vermont with his wife, daughter, three cats, two dogs, and a rabbit. He writes in a messy office in his basement, and when he isn't working, he likes to ski, skate, hike in the woods, kayak on the lake, take photographs, and read.

APPENDIX

HANK GREENBERG CAREER STATISTICS

FULL NAME: Henry Benjamin Greenberg

BORN: January 1, 1911 in New York, New York **DEATH:** September 4, 1986

HEIGHT: 6'3" **WEIGHT:** 210 lbs. **BATS:** Right **THROWS:** Right

YEAR	TEAM	GAMES	AB	RUNS	HITS	HR	RBI	AVG
1930	Detroit	1	1	0	0	0	0	.000
1933	Detroit	117	449	59	135	12	87	.301
1934	Detroit	153	593	118	201	26	139	.339
1935	Detroit	152	619	121	203	36	170	.328
1936	Detroit	12	46	10	16	1	16	.348
1937	Detroit	154	594	137	200	40	183	.337
1938	Detroit	155	556	144	175	58	146	.315
1939	Detroit	138	500	112	156	33	112	.340
1940	Detroit	148	573	129	195	41	150	.340
1941	Detroit	19	67	12	18	2	12	.269
1945	Detroit	78	270	47	84	13	60	.311
1946	Detroit	142	523	91	145	44	127	.277
1947	Pittsburgh	125	402	71	100	25	74	.249
TOTAL		1,394	5,193	1,051	1,648	331	1,276	.313

JACKIE ROBINSON CAREER STATISTICS

FULL NAME: Jack Roosevelt Robinson

BORN: January 31, 1919 in Cairo, Georgia **DEATH:** October 24, 1972

HEIGHT: 5'11" **WEIGHT:** 204 lbs. **BATS:** Right **THROWS:** Right

YEAR	TEAM	GAMES	AB	RUNS	HITS	HR	RBI	AVG
1947	Brooklyn	151	590	125	175	12	48	.297
1948	Brooklyn	147	574	108	170	12	85	.296
1949	Brooklyn	156	593	122	203	16	124	.342
1950	Brooklyn	144	518	99	170	14	81	.328
1951	Brooklyn	153	548	106	185	19	88	.338
1952	Brooklyn	149	510	104	157	19	75	.308
1953	Brooklyn	136	484	109	159	12	95	.329
1954	Brooklyn	124	386	62	120	15	39	.311
1955	Brooklyn	105	317	51	81	8	36	.256
1956	Brooklyn	117	357	61	98	10	43	.275
TOTAL		1,382	4,877	947	1,518	137	734	.311

FERNANDO VALENZUELA CAREER STATISTICS

FULL NAME: Fernando Valenzuela

BORN: November 1, 1960 in Etchohuaquila, Mexico

HEIGHT: 5'11" **WEIGHT:** 195 lbs. **BATS:** Left **THROWS:** Left

YEAR	TEAM	G	W	L	IP	ERA
1980	LA Dodgers	10	2	0	17.2	0.00
1981	LA Dodgers	25	13	7	192.1	2.48
1982	LA Dodgers	37	19	13	285.0	2.87
1983	LA Dodgers	35	15	10	257.0	3.75
1984	LA Dodgers	34	12	17	261.0	3.03
1985	LA Dodgers	35	17	10	272.1	2.45
1986	LA Dodgers	34	21	11	269.1	3.14
1987	LA Dodgers	34	14	14	251.0	3.98
1988	LA Dodgers	23	5	8	142.1	4.24
1989	LA Dodgers	31	10	13	196.2	3.43
1990	LA Dodgers	33	13	13	204.0	4.59
1991	Angels	2	0	2	6.2	12.15
1993	Baltimore	32	8	10	178.2	4.94
1994	Philadelphia	8	1	2	45.0	3.00
1995	San Diego	29	8	3	90.1	4.98
1996	San Diego	33	13	8	171.2	3.62
1997	San Diego	13	2	8	66.1	4.75
1997	St. Louis	5	0	4	22.2	5.56
TOTAL		453	173	153	2,930	3.54

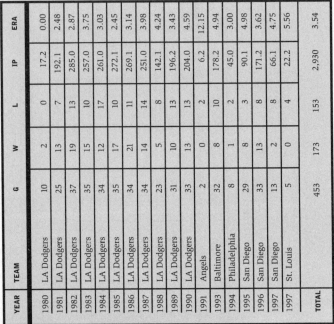

ILA BORDERS CAREER STATISTICS

FULL NAME: Ila Borders

BORN: February 18, 1975

HEIGHT: 5'10" **WEIGHT:** 160 lbs. **BATS:** Left **THROWS:** Left

YEAR	TEAM	G	W	L	IP	ERA
1997	St. Paul	7	0	0	6	7.50
1997	Duluth	8	0	0	8.1	7.56
1998	Duluth	14	1	4	43.2	8.66
1999	Duluth	3	0	0	2.1	30.86
1999	Madison	12	1	0	32.1	1.67
2000	Zion	5	0	0	8.2	8.31
TOTAL		52	2	4	101.1	6.75